FIT FOR THE PULPIT

fit for the pulpit

THE PREACHER & HIS CHALLENGES

CHRIS McCURLEY, EDITOR

featuring:

CHRIS MCCURLEY

NEAL POLLARD

JACOB HAWK

JAY LOCKHART

JEFF A. JENKINS

ADAM FAUGHN

DALE JENKINS

KIRK BROTHERS

MICHAEL WHITWORTH

STEVE HIGGINBOTHAM

START2FINISH

ISBN 978-0-615-92520-2 (softcover)
ISBN 978-0-9885121-3-9 (ebook)

Library of Congress Control Number 2013956163

Published by Start2Finish
Bend, Oregon 97702
start2finish.org

Printed in the United States of America

27 26 25 24 23   2 3 4 5 6

Cover Design by Evangela Creative

contents

introduction

Where there are people, there are problems. The church is not exempt from this truth. Problems exist and, at times, persist because people are present. We humans have a tendency to get in our own way. We find it easy to make mountains out of molehills or shoot ourselves in the foot. The church should function as a city of refuge from the inconsistencies and travesties of the world. But all too often, worldly problems infiltrate the church because of the personalities behind them. Many Christians experience devastating grief and profound pain. It is the responsibility of the brethren to assist these hurting individuals in an effort to help them overcome. However, many problems that present themselves within the confines of the church are less than monumental, yet they nevertheless cause undue stress. Most shepherds in a local congregation spend vast amounts of time dealing with issues that are more trivial than tragic. Many times, the preacher receives the brunt of these problems; because he is a high-profile person in the church, he is also an easy target for those wishing to shout their displeasure.

Some preachers beg for criticism by the way they function in their God-given role. When a minister of the gospel does not take his responsibility seriously, he can and should expect disapproval. There is no reason for God's preacher to be lazy, arrogant, or unreliable. It is a disgrace to the pulpit and to the church when the preacher approaches the work half-heartedly. The church needs men of God who seek to imitate Christ before they ever step into the pulpit. We are Christians first!

Preaching is not for the faint of heart. It is not like any other profession. It is mentally taxing, emotionally draining, and physically exhausting. But it is also spiritually rewarding. To be a preacher in the Lord's church is both trying and tremendous. It is both difficult and delightful. It is juxtaposition between grueling and glorious. At times, we may be able to sympathize with Jeremiah: "For whenever I speak, I cry out, I shout, 'Violence and destruction!' For the word of the LORD has become for me a reproach and derision all day long" (Jer. 20:8). Such "reproach and derision" should never deter us. Like Paul, we should not be ashamed of the gospel "for it is the power of God for salvation to everyone who believes" (Rom. 1:16). There is too much at stake for the preacher to bow out of service. No matter how treacherous the trade of ministry becomes, it is vital that we press on and persist in proclaiming God's Word. The preacher has the unique ability and extraordinary opportunity to make an eternal difference in the lives of others. May we never allow discouragement to extinguish the fire in our bones (Jer. 20:9).

The purpose of this book is to assist the preacher with some of the more common problems presented in ministry. All too often, preachers leave the pulpit, the ministry, or even the church because of the hardships associated with church work. I cannot help but think that some of these men might still be serving today if they had been equipped to handle such problems. It is my hope and prayer that this book will be a "self-help manual" for all preachers, young and old alike, who ask the question, "Who ministers to the minister?" My desire is for it to be encouraging and motivating while, at the same time, instructional. I have asked nine bulwarks of preaching to write from biblical teaching and personal experience concerning how to handle potential complications in local church ministry. May the reader find solace in the fact that he is not on an island when it comes to coping with such issues. Let us work to rise above the problems to accomplish the ultimate goal.

God bless the preacher!

— Chris McCurley

.

the preacher & his time
chris mccurley

A Fortune 500 company wanted to manage their time more effectively, so they hired an expert in the subject to conduct a seminar. The expert lectured for two hours and then summarized his presentation through the use of visual aid. He placed a large, clear, open-mouthed jar in front of the group of executives. He then placed seven large rocks in the jar. He asked, "Is the jar full?" Everyone nodded in the affirmative.

Then the expert took a cup of pebbles and poured them into the jar until they touched the rim. He asked again, "Is the jar full?" No one responded. Next, he took a cup of fine sand and poured it into the jar. "Is it completely full now?" he asked, and a few executives, not really sure of the answer, nodded half-heartedly. The expert then took water and poured into the jar, filling it to the top. "Now the jar is full," he stated.

He concluded his little demonstration by asking the question, "What does this lesson teach us about time management?" Everyone's hand shot up, and one executive replied, "It teaches us that no matter how busy you are, you can always fit more things into your schedule." "WRONG!" the expert shot back. "The lesson," he said, "Is this: unless you put the big rocks in first, they will never fit. Each and every one of you must determine what the big rocks are for you."[1]

All of us are responsible for how we spend God's time. Every minute of every day is either wasted or wisely invested. Paul wrote, "Look carefully then how you walk, not as unwise but as wise, making the best use of the time, because the days are evil" (Eph. 5:15–16). Time is a non-renewable resource. Our world certainly understands this, which is why it has invented all sorts of timesaving devices and time-management strategies. However, time cannot truly be managed. It cannot be saved for later. We cannot slow it down or speed it up. All we can do is make the most of the blessing we have been given. Time is not ours to do with as we please. Though we often speak of time in ownership terms, time does not belong to us. We are but stewards of the time God has gifted to us; therefore, we must invest it wisely.

We must redeem it.

Time management can prove incredibly difficult for the preacher. There is one unavoidable truth for the one who mans the pulpit each Lord's Day—Sunday is coming! If writing and delivering a sermon were the only duties a preacher had to fulfill, then time management would be much less of an issue. Alas, preachers work to meet a Sunday deadline while visiting the hospital, counseling the hurting, teaching Bible classes, conducting Bible studies, writing a bulletin article, leading a devotional, and raising a family. Some preachers have the benefit of working with a staff that can shoulder some of the load, but many minsters find themselves in churches where they

---

1. Stephen Covey, A. Roger Merrill, Rebecca R. Merrill, *First Things First* (New York: Free Press, 1994), 88–89.

are a staff of one. Regardless of whether one is alone or part of a staff, he still must manage his time wisely and effectively. Time is valuable for the preacher—more valuable than money. He must therefore learn to strike a balance between his ministerial duties, his home life, and his personal study.

the good start

My father used to say, "Find a job you love, and you will never work a day in your life." Preaching is a job I dearly love, but make no mistake: it is work. Some claim that preaching is more than an occupation; it is a lifestyle. I would agree. However, we must not allow the work of ministry to consume us to the point that we are absentee fathers, neglectful husbands, or immature Christians. We must determine what the "big rocks" are in our lives and put them in our jar first. The biggest rock is God. Our relationship with *the* Rock should be the most important thing in our lives.

There is no question that Jesus was a busy man. He taught, preached, healed, fed the multitudes, and exorcised demons. He faced the constant pressure of people seeking to take him by force. Think about the throngs of people pressing in on him, falling at his feet, pleading for a miracle. Being the Messiah and doing the work of the Father was very demanding. Yet Jesus never let the pace of life deter him from what was most important. Jesus was never so busy that he lost focus. Take note of a few passages that illustrate Jesus' commitment to what was most important:

> Rising very early in the morning, while it was still dark, he departed and went out to a desolate place, and there he prayed.
>
> Mark 1:35

When it was day, he departed and went into a desolate place. And the people sought him and came to him, and would have kept him from leaving them.

Luke 4:42

Perceiving then that they were about to come and take him by force to make him king, Jesus withdrew again to the mountain by himself.

John 6:15

He would withdraw to desolate places and pray.

Luke 5:16

Jesus began his ministry with forty days of solitude, and throughout his life, he always made time to be alone with the Father. The question becomes, if Jesus needed to break away from the rigors of daily ministry, how much more do we?

Now as they went on their way, Jesus entered a village. And a woman named Martha welcomed him into her house. And she had a sister called Mary, who sat at the Lord's feet and listened to his teaching. But Martha was distracted with much serving. And she went up to him and said, "Lord, do you not care that my sister has left me to serve alone? Tell her then to help me." But the Lord answered her, "Martha, Martha, you are anxious and troubled about many things, but one thing is necessary. Mary has chosen the good portion, which will not be taken away from her."

Luke 10:38–42

To have Jesus come to your house for a meal would be a monumental event indeed. One can understand why Martha was scurrying about to make certain that all of the preparations and arrangements were precise. She wanted to impress her guests, but despite her sincere efforts, she lost sight of what was most important. The beast of busyness had locked its arms tightly around her, and when one is caught in the clutches of this beast, it leads to stress and frustration. Notice again Martha's words: "Lord, do you not care that my sister has left me to serve alone? Tell her then to help me." Martha was annoyed at her sister because she wouldn't help her with the preparations, and she was annoyed at Jesus because he wouldn't come to her aid and rebuke Mary for sitting down when there was work to be done. "Do you not care?" she asks Jesus. Our Lord kindly rebukes Martha by claiming that, while the chore she was engaged in was important, she was more concerned than the situation demanded. The meal was not a big rock. As far as priority, Mary had chosen the best thing. She had taken time to pause and sit at Jesus' feet.

Being busy doesn't ensure productivity. One can spend every waking minute of their lives being busy, but not accomplish much of anything. The preacher cannot be so consumed with "the meal" that he fails to sit at Jesus' feet. A lot of things are important, but only one thing is most important. The local preacher's primary responsibility is to preaching; therefore, he must give the proper amount of time and attention to study of God's Word. Unfortunately, some elderships and members alike thrust tasks upon the preacher that should not be solely his. For instance, while I feel strongly that the preacher should be involved in visitation, he should not be the only one in the congregation carrying out this duty. Elders should visit. Christians should visit.

The same is true for evangelism. The Great Commission is

for all, not just the preacher. Again, I feel strongly that the local preacher should be dedicated to studying with individuals, but all too often, elders and church members exclude themselves from this vital work, relying instead on the preacher to do it for them. I have seen too many preachers leave the pulpit due to burnout. Oftentimes, this could have been avoided had the leadership and the members sought to assist the minister. I had a friend who preached for a relatively small congregation in southwest Missouri. His weekly duties consisted of preaching Sunday morning and evening, teaching Bible classes on Sunday and Wednesday, teaching a ladies Bible class on Tuesday, delivering the Wednesday night devotional, printing the bulletin, officiating weddings and funerals, personal evangelism, and answering the phone. This was a church that had plenty of able-bodied members to lift some of the burden from this poor preacher, but they chose to sit idly by while he struggled to meet the demands of the job.

There is a great chasm between idealism and realism. Ideally, I would love to see churches work *with* the preacher instead of expecting the preacher to work *for* them. But because we live in reality, I understand some churches do not operate this way and, as such, some preachers will struggle with giving time and attention to what matters most. What the preacher cannot do is allow maturing his faith to take a backseat to the demands of church work. I am confident that any preacher (and any person for that matter) will find that when they get God right, they get everything else right. I heard a preacher say once, "The main thing is to keep the main thing the main thing." Jesus certainly validates that statement.

home is where the start is

There is another relationship that must take precedence over the preacher's work, and that is his relationship with his family. The Great Commission starts at home. How many times have we witnessed a dynamic preacher with spiritually depraved children? We cannot afford to become so wrapped up in serving the church that we fail to serve our family. Second only to our relationship with God is our relationship with our spouse and children. There will be times when we will be called to sit with a grieving family at the hospital late at night, or meet with individuals for spiritual counseling or Bible study "after hours." Some elders will call meetings in the evening and, the preacher is required to attend. There are certain situations that pull us away from the home that cannot be avoided. But aside from these instances, we must be diligent not to allow our responsibilities as a preacher to override our responsibilities at home. Remember Paul's words:

> Husbands, love your wives, as Christ loved the church and gave himself up for her, that he might sanctify her, having cleansed her by the washing of water with the word, so that he might present the church to himself in splendor, without spot or wrinkle or any such thing, that she might be holy and without blemish. In the same way husbands should love their wives as their own bodies. He who loves his wife loves himself. For no one ever hated his own flesh, but nourishes and cherishes it, just as Christ does the church, because we are members of his body. "Therefore a man shall leave his father and mother and hold fast to his wife, and the two shall become one flesh." This mystery is profound, and I am saying that it refers

to Christ and the church. However, let each one
of you love his wife as himself, and let the wife
see that she respects her husband.

Eph. 5:25–33

Paul illustrated the strict importance of the husband meeting
the needs of his wife. Husbands are to love their wives "as their
own bodies." To love your wife as your own body certainly
requires that she be a top priority in your life. Marriage is God's
divine design. In the beginning, God looked upon the loneliness
of man and determined that his solitude was not good. In
response, he fashioned woman from one of Adam's ribs (Gen.
2:21–22). She was the perfect complement to him; not only that,
she completed man. She was his helper (Gen. 2:18).

Therefore a man shall leave his father and his
mother and hold fast to his wife, and they shall
become one flesh. And the man and his wife were
both naked and were not ashamed.

Gen. 2:24–25

Pertaining to the subject of marriage, Jesus taught "What
therefore God has joined together, let not man separate" (Matt.
19:6). The imagery of husband and wife being joined together,
becoming one flesh and inseparable, leaves no doubt as to
the importance of this sacred relationship. Is it possible for
the preacher to allow his work to separate him from his wife?
Absolutely! Although the work of a minister is godly work,
Satan can easily use it to his advantage. The preacher should be
concerned, but not consumed. He should be a hard-worker, but
not a workaholic. He must be dedicated to the Lord's church,
but not disloyal to his family.

"Behold, children are a heritage from the LORD, the fruit

of the womb a reward" (Psa. 127:3). Children are a blessing from God; we all recognize that. But we sometimes do a poor job of demonstrating that. Incidentally, "heritage" in Psa. 127:3 is the Hebrew *nahalah*, meaning "possession," "property," or "inheritance." Gifts are meant to be treasured and cherished. The best way to treasure and cherish our children is to return them to their rightful owner. We are stewards of every blessing God has bestowed upon us, including our children. Being a *good* parent is about being a *godly* parent.

Successful parenting begins and ends with giving our children back to God. Like Hannah, we too should give them to the Lord all the days of their life (1 Sam. 1:11). Psalm 127 continues: "Like arrows in the hand of a warrior are the children of one's youth" (v. 4). What does one do with an arrow? You aim it at a target and let it fly. If our children are like arrows, then we should be aiming them at a target and firing them toward the bull's eye. That bull's eye, of course, is heaven, and we do not get points for getting close. It is an all-or-nothing proposition, meaning we cannot afford to allow anything to hinder us. As important and critical as our work is, preaching does not trump parenting.

One of the beauties of ministry is that it allows for family involvement. There doesn't always have to be a clear line of demarcation between ministry and family. In fact, the two can often be blended. Our wives can be a vital resource in our work. Our children need to see us modeling a commitment and dedication to the Lord's church. Involving the family in your work can pay major dividends in maintaining a healthy marriage and raising godly children.

the rest

A wise minister once told me that a preacher should spend

a minimum of twenty hours a week on his sermon. This means, of course, that if you preach twice on Sunday, at least forty hours each week should be spent on sermon preparation. While I greatly respected him, I did not agree with his assessment. The preacher's role within the church is to preach. This role must be fulfilled first. However, the preacher should not spend all his time holed up in the office. Some preachers come in early, close the door, and never emerge until the day is over. While I'm sure they are using that time to construct meaningful sermons, they also may be neglecting certain duties like visiting the sick, studying with prospective disciples, and consulting the spiritually ill. I have heard a preacher say from the pulpit, "Don't expect me to visit you if you are in the hospital. That's not my job. That's the elders' responsibility." While I don't totally disagree with that sentiment (although a little tact would have been in order), the preacher should serve the congregation in ways other than simply standing behind the pulpit.

What tends to happen with some ministers is that they spend an inordinate amount of time engaging in tasks that are ancillary to their primary responsibility—preaching. It is often the case, when this occurs, that the preacher will scurry around on Saturday evening and forfeit family time to work up a lesson to preach the next day. As a result, the lesson is typically not afforded the proper time and attention since the preacher must hurry to prepare it.

Without a doubt, there will be occasions when the preacher is called to sit with a grieving family until the wee hours of the morning, or spends many hours waiting in the hospital while a member has emergency surgery. Some things are unforeseen and cannot help but cut into sermon prep time. Virtually every preacher has had the unenviable task of staying up late or getting up extra early to meet the deadline of preaching on Sunday. Any man who preaches for an extended period of time will face the difficulty of managing time when it seems to be running short. However, in the absence of unexpected events, we can greatly lessen our stress level by utilizing a bit of strategy. Allow me to offer a few suggestions to assist the preacher in managing his time:

Stick to a schedule. In most congregations, the elders do not put the preacher on a time clock—he doesn't have to clock in and out, but can come and go as he pleases. It can be easy to take advantage of such freedom. In fact, some ministers do, and it ends up biting them in the end. Have a weekly and daily routine. When possible, get to the office at the same time every day. Set a goal each day of what you want to accomplish. Obviously, sermon preparation should be at the top of the list; schedule activities accordingly. Have a day set aside for visiting. Schedule a certain day and time for counseling or meeting individuals for Bible study. If you have a secretary, you may tell her to take messages during the morning hours so that you can study uninterrupted. There are some people who can fly by the seat of their pants and make it work. Most of us, however, need a plan. Organization is a vital tool for the preacher. Customize your day and week in a fashion that allows you to fulfill the duties on your schedule.

Work ahead. "What am I going to preach on Sunday?" It's a question every preacher is confronted with every single week. One thing that has helped me immensely in my life as a preacher is working ahead; e.g. planning sermons weeks or months in advance. Personally, I try to stay at least two months ahead on sermons. I know preachers who are a year ahead. Some sit down at the end of the year and plan what they will preach in the year to come. This isn't easy to implement in the short-term, but it will pay huge dividends long-term. Working ahead allows for less stress when the unexpected interferes with one's regular routine. The preacher's week is made easier when he enters into it knowing what he's going to preach on the following Sunday. By working ahead, he can greatly reduce (or even eliminate) the angst that comes from working on a deadline.

Learn to say, "No!" Time management must include the ability to say "No!" to some things. The preacher cannot do everything, even though some in the congregation may expect him to. A vital word in the preacher's vocabulary is that little word, "No!" Many things are important, but not everything is a priority or a must. Church members will always feel as though their wants, needs, or ideas should garner the utmost attention. Undoubtedly, they will be frustrated, even angry, when the preacher does not agree. However, the minister cannot cater to every want, meet every need, or foster every idea. It is unrealistic for the members to expect him to do so. The preacher is not at the church's complete disposal. He is at God's complete disposal, which means he first must fulfill the biblical obligation to "preach the word" and "be ready in season and out of season; reprove, rebuke, and exhort, with complete patience and teaching" (2 Tim. 4:2). Saying "No!" isn't easy. It will not always be well received, but it is an invaluable term in the preacher's vernacular. It's possible for one to work so diligently to please everyone that he ends up pleasing no one.

Don't be afraid to ask for help. It's not a show of weakness for the preacher to seek assistance. If he is feeling stressed out, maxed out, or burned out, he should go to his elders and speak to them about getting some relief. I have known too many preachers who were spread too thin or stretched to the limit, and one day they snap. Rather than expressing their woes to the shepherds, they suppress their stress. It is common for an eldership to be somewhat disconnected from what the preacher faces on a daily basis. Some are unaware of how demanding preaching can be. Is it possible for a group of shepherds to be unrealistic when it comes to the amount of work they expect from the preacher? Elders should be able to recognize when their preacher has too much on his plate. The preacher should not be expected to do the work of an elder or deacon, nor should he be expected to shoulder the entire load when it comes to evangelism, visitation, teaching Bible class, leading devotionals, etc. If the preacher feels as though there are not enough hours in the week to accomplish what he has been assigned, then it's time to have a heart-to-heart meeting with the shepherds to make them aware of his concerns. He needs to be at his best. He can be greatly hindered in this effort if he feels overwhelmed.

I had a member ask me one time, "So what do you do the rest of the week?" This sweet lady assumed that I only worked on Sunday. Oh, if she only knew! Most people are unaware or unconcerned about the preacher's role aside from preaching— that is, until they need something from him. Regardless of what he had to deal with during the week, members still expect him to hit a home run on Sunday. Delivering a quality sermon doesn't just happen. It takes hours of preparation. It takes determined devotion. It takes a conscientious commitment. Other things are always vying for the preacher's time. Many of these things are important. At times, they may even take precedence over sermon preparation. It can be a difficult balancing act. Juggling multiple responsibilities while working to meet a looming deadline can make one weary and worn. Preaching is not for the faint of heart. It takes a man after God's own heart; one who meets the challenges of being God's instrument head on; one who redeems the time that he has been blessed with by investing it in a relationship with God, family, and ministry.

One of the greatest challenges everyone in life faces is putting the big rocks in the jar first. Too many times, we fill our jar with the smaller things—things that may be important, but not *most* important. Therefore, we face a constant battle, the fight to not let the lighter things squeeze out the weightier things. We cannot make our jar bigger or the rocks smaller. The only option is to put the large rocks in first. Time management is not about seeing how many things you can squeeze into your jar. It's about making what's most important fit!

2

the preacher &
his relationships
neal pollard

Try as hard as he might, it is difficult for the preacher to think about his daily life without thinking in terms of people. As he looks back over his weekly schedule, the preacher will remember conversations with widows, counseling sessions, various meetings, hospital and in-home visitation, writing visitor letters, evangelistic studies and follow-ups with new Christians, funerals, weddings, and time at home with his family. The life of a preacher is a life in constant contact with people. It's difficult to think of the preacher's life apart from relationships.

Jesus, the greatest preacher the world has ever known, invested heavily and regularly in relationships. Wherever one reads in the gospels, he sees this fact. Consider a random selection of Scripture, Luke 17:11–19:10, that reveals the life of Christ as he dealt with people.

- He related to sick people (Luke 17:11–19), showing us that the sick will often be isolated, that they need attention, regardless of how they respond, and that there will always be those grateful for our efforts.

- He related to young people (Luke 18:15–17), showing us the value of being in their lives for the good.

- He related to unreceptive people (Luke 18:18–25), showing us that they may seem like good soil, but are hindered by greater loyalty to something else, and are wrestling with a formidable foe.

- He related to struggling people (Luke 18:35–43), showing us that people search when needy, that such people are in need of mercy, and that such people need only what Christ can give.

- He related to lost people (Luke 19:1–10), showing us that lost people are often unsavory, often cannot see Christ for the crowd, may be people that others can see no potential in, and are often people who are willing to repent.

- He related to the Lord's people (Luke 17–19), teaching them, communicating with them, and urging them to live right.

It seems Christ was constantly investing in one relationship or another, and this was despite the fact that he was unmarried and without children.

From that brief examination of Jesus' life and work, we are impressed that ministry will be about people and relationships. He shows us that some relationships will be much more pleasant than others. All relationships will have high and low points. In each relationship, we must ask ourselves if we are holding up our end of the deal—something Jesus always did to a perfect degree, and we will not. But the preacher who looks intently at his life and does what is right in terms of relationships goes a long way toward both personal satisfaction and effectiveness in ministry.

the preacher & the world

In a recent chapel talk at the Bear Valley Bible Institute of Denver, Dr. Stafford North preached from Luke 10:25–29. This text records a statement from a certain man who was an expert in the Law of Moses. The text gives Jesus' response and reveals the man's follow-up, self-justifying question: "Who is my neighbor?" That question gives rise to Jesus' parable of the Good Samaritan. Dr. North made the point that we often apply that parable to those far away who need our help. While that is not a wrong application, how often do we neglect or ignore our literal neighbors and the people with whom we have daily interaction?

Dr. North challenged those present, nearly everyone a preacher, to get to know our neighbors, maybe invite them for dinner. As we get to know them, we should serve them as their needs become known. Ultimately, such paves the way for us to study with them. Dr. North asked us to dream of what could be if every member of the church in this nation got to know, serve, and ultimately engage all their neighbors for the sake of the gospel. What would that do to their view of Christ and Christianity? How deeply would that impact church growth?

To "do the work of an evangelist" (2 Tim. 4:5) requires the preacher to establish and develop relationships with people in the world. It is easy for the preacher to sequester himself in his office and limit his contacts to members and anyone else who happens to venture inside the church building. Evangelism is becoming harder in a world that seems more interested in keeping to itself, rather than making time and giving effort to build relationships. It is also as easy as striking up friendships with neighbors, postal workers, clerks, doctors, dentists, insurance agents, mechanics, family members of our brethren… the list is endless! It is good for the preacher to be exemplary to the congregation in this regard, living out what Jesus says about being salt and light (Matt. 5:13–16). That is what Christ wants of his people, especially of someone so influential to church-life as is the preacher. A better world, nation, community, and neighborhood is as simple as Christ being in the lives of the lost all around us. The preacher plays an incredibly important role in this.

the preacher & the local church

As we observed in Luke 17–19, Jesus took quite a bit of time to be with his disciples. From the time of its establishment, the early church modeled a togetherness that was undoubtedly a part of its rapid growth. Paul's letters to Timothy, especially 1 Timothy, reveals the relationship that should exist between the preacher and the various members of the local church. While the apostle spends a great deal of time talking about how the church should function (e.g. leadership, gender roles, widows, wealthy members), he also discusses how Timothy, the preacher, ought to conduct himself among the members of the Ephesian church.

It makes good common sense to suggest that the preacher must form healthy, strong relationships with his brethren. One of the important functions of hospital visits, visiting the elderly, practicing hospitality, being present and involved in fellowship activities, workdays, attending kids' games, counseling, and more is their role in fostering relationships with the church.

Relationships at the macro level. There is a legitimate sense in which we are everyone's preacher. We do not belong to a particular age group, income bracket, political ideology, interest group, or clique. How harmful if we cater to a group or neglect a certain demographic! There will always be those with whom we share a greater affinity, while others will be harder to get to know, talk to, or otherwise engage. But our focus should be on being accessible and helpful to everyone—not just a few.

Relationships with close friends. In times past, preaching students were counseled to avoid having close relationships. The concept behind the counsel probably aligns with the comments above about being everybody's preacher. Yet when I observe the life of Christ, I see him spending extra time alone with Peter, James, John, and sometimes Andrew. John even autobiographically referred to himself as the disciple whom Jesus loved (e.g. John 20:2). Inasmuch as other members of the church enjoy the prerogative of close friendship, the preacher should be afforded the same privilege. But he should remember some important caveats:

- Do not be cliquish, whether at services or regarding personal time away from the building. If you spend most of your social time with the same few people, it will show and negatively impact your ministry.

- Do not be exclusive, keeping others from fellowship or social activities.

- Do not overly invest in a few families to the neglect of the whole church. If they move or the relationship cools or sours, the preacher and his family can find himself "out on an island," estranged from the majority.

- Do not completely ignore any complaints from members that you are being cliquish. While the criticism might come from a cranky, cantankerous member, could there be some truth to it?

- Do not lose your evangelistic edge, cordoning off all free time with friends to the exclusion of non-members.
- Do not lose your hospitality edge, having the same few families into your house to the exclusion of the majority.

Being able to enjoy the holidays, vacations, regular outings, or events with special friends can enrich one's personal satisfaction in ministry. Some people may not enjoy time with you at the ballpark, in the duck blind, on the hiking trails, on the lake, in the campground, at the symphony, or wherever you enjoy spending your time. Cultivate these special relationships, knowing that these provide special memories for you and your family.

Relationships with new and fringe members. By the time I was in my first local work, I had lived in a total of twelve cities in four states. My dad had done both domestic mission work and local work with self-supporting congregations, and I learned quickly how to adapt to new environments. While I had a lot of practice with starting over in a new place, it always presented the challenge of starting anew. Today, more and more people tend to move and live in multiple communities during their formidable years. More of us know how that "new kid on the block" syndrome feels. The preacher must model, not only acceptance, but proactively search for ways to incorporate new and loosely-attached/unattached members. Divorcees, singles, single parents, children and teens from broken homes, widows and widowers—all these can feel disenfranchised. Pay attention to the lonely and lowly; Jesus did (Mark 10:46; John 4:7).

the preacher & the elders

The lengthiest discussion in Scripture between a preacher

and an eldership takes place in Acts 20; it involves Paul and the elders at Ephesus. While this does not exactly parallel today's local-work environment, it is worth our notice. Paul sends for these elders to meet him in Miletus. He looks back over their relationship that had lasted at least three years. It was characterized by:

- relationship (v. 18)
- humility (v. 19)
- emotion (v. 31)
- his assisting them in their private and public work (v. 20)
- their having done church work together (v. 25)
- willingness to challenge them and even admonish them (vv. 27–31)
- mutual affection and respect (vv. 32–35)

To me, the most important proof of their relationship was what we see when they parted company. "And when he had said these things, he knelt down and prayed with them all. And there was much weeping on the part of all; they embraced Paul and kissed him, being sorrowful most of all because of the word he had spoken, that they would not see his face again. And they accompanied him to the ship" (Acts 20:36–38). Why do we not experience more of this between elders and preachers today? Instead of being competitors, rivals, or adversaries, we should all be men who love each other enough to build strong relationships.

With elders, I have played tennis, basketball, softball, and pranks at church camp in the middle of the night. I've traveled with them on vacations and mission trips, attended lectureships and seminars. That does not mean I have always seen eye-to-eye with them on judgment calls, plans, proposals, and priorities. But at the end of the day, there should be a fierce loyalty, galvanized by love and respect, that ties us together. Mutual communication, commendation, and cooperation are three ingredients in the recipe for a happy preacher-elder relationship.

the preacher & the difficult

The late Wendell Winkler, in his course *Preacher & His Work*, taught a section entitled "Meet the Congregation." The premise behind the lecture was that we will encounter difficult people in our ministries wherever we find ourselves. That last part was important, that the same people (though the faces, names, shapes, and sizes will change) were in every congregation where we could work. Here are some of those people we encounter in the local church.

- Mr./Mrs. Come on strong (they are quick to be your friend)
- Mr./Mrs. "What this church needs"
- Mr./Mrs. Occupy all your time telling you all their troubles
- Mr./Mrs. Gigger (they push your buttons)
- Mr./Mrs. "Have you been to see _____?"
- Mr./Mrs. Always correcting (e.g. grammar, the bulletin)
- Mr./Mrs. Never commend you
- Mr./Mrs. "What/how you spend your time"
- Mr./Mrs. "We need a sermon on…"
- Mr./Mrs. Ask questions to no benefit
- Mr./Mrs. "Brother Jones, our former preacher…"

- Mr./Mrs. Chip on the shoulder
- Mr./Mrs. "We're not getting equal time"

Bro. Winkler's overarching point was that nearly everyone in the congregation would be such a joy to work with, and that loving and appreciating these people was no chore, but that there would also be problem-people. In my three local works, my assessment would certainly echo that thought. I have encountered these difficult personalities everywhere I have been. How do you work on relationships with difficult people?

Discharge your duty. Even when there are difficult personalities to cope with, you must still "fulfill your ministry" (2 Tim. 4:5). Notice that Paul, in the same verse, mentions enduring unspecified afflictions. It's easy to simply avoid problem people, but we need to seek out ways to show them Christ's love. That does not require subjecting ourselves to unreasonable behavior. But at times, this will amount to turning our cheeks (Matt. 5:39). Show them the love of Christ. Who knows but that your example might influence them to improve their behavior toward you?

Do your part. You are not accountable for their attitude and actions, but you are accountable for your own. How terrible to allow subtle sins—gossip, bitterness, outbursts of anger, worry, fear—to overtake you when encountering a difficult person. What can you do when facing a problem personality? Smile, be kind, serve them, and practice gentleness. Consider the inspired advice Paul gave a young preacher,

> The Lord's servant must not be quarrelsome but kind to everyone, able to teach, patiently enduring evil, correcting his opponents with gentleness. God may perhaps grant them repentance leading to a knowledge of the truth, and they may come

to their senses and escape from the snare of the
devil, after being captured by him to do his will.

2 Tim. 2:24–26

Remember the old adage, "Hurt people hurt people."
Allen Webster shared that with me. Those hurting in some way
tend to lash out at others. Understanding this might engender
sympathy for, or at least understanding of, their difficult-to-
handle behavior. People carry incredibly heavy burdens: hurt,
guilt, loss, depression, disappointment. Many of the people to
whom we try to minister are broken. While some bear these
burdens gracefully, others lash out in pain. It is encouraging to
consider how Allen said he handles the eruptions of hurt people
he encounters. He said he is thankful that the hurtful response is
aimed at him if it means a weak, new, or non-Christian is spared
this ugly reaction. What a positive and spiritual plan of action!
With Christ living in us and God strengthening us, we can bear
up under unfair treatment (cf. 1 Pet. 2:20; 3:14).

Remember that the bulk of your interactions with people
will be at worst neutral. But more often, they will be positive
and beneficial. When difficult people cross our paths, we need
to understand it as an inevitable part of interchange with people.
Such experiences are often opportunities in disguise. We need
wisdom and maturity not to run or retaliate, but rather respond
in Christlikeness.

Through the years, I have had negative and difficult
experiences with people: the suicidal, drug addicts,
murderers, homosexuals, those in marital distress, the sick and
dying, the disorderly, and those facing heartbreaking tragedy.
I've also had an abundance of wonderful memories involving

people: unlikely conversions, aiding brethren as they grew to be deacons, elders, preachers, and missionaries, working with orphans, widows, and teens, witnessing atheists becoming believers, seeing the disfellowshipped return and repent, and being exposed to some of the best people in the world! Most preachers would be hard-pressed to relinquish any such interactions, as all of them help the preacher in some way as he continues to deal with people.

As a preacher, I have learned this about most people:

- Most people want love and attention. Be empathetic!
- Most people have the capacity to do the right thing, believe it or not.
- Most people will respond to kind, respectful interaction. But be patient.
- Most people can be misunderstood. Give them the benefit of the doubt.
- Most people behave poorer when they are having a bad day.
- Most people are not out to get you. Avoid paranoia.
- Most people are open to doing the right thing.
- Most people are struggling with the same fundamental problems and fears.
- Most people can learn to be team players, though they may need to be coached.
- Most people value the idea of community.

You will not preach very long without a love for people. Some preachers seem to believe preaching only requires one to know how to write and deliver sermons and Bible classes. While preparation and delivery are crucial to success as a preacher, a man will not be effective in the pulpit if he is isolated from the people. The longer I preach, the more I realize the importance of people in my life as a preacher, whether listening sympathetically as they reveal heartbreaking stories (though I may have dozens of other things to do), pleading with them to obey the gospel (knowing they will spend eternity elsewhere), or finding out they struggle with deep, dark temptations that overwhelm them. I do not know how many times I have heard about a preacher being asked to resign or being fired, not for his preaching, but because of what was going on when he was not preaching—he was aloof, uninvolved in the life of the congregation, and unwilling to develop relationships with people.

Some people treat us worse than we deserve, but more treat us better. We must make the deliberate decision to love, serve, help, encourage, and believe in all of them, and do what we can to help them get to heaven. Every moment we spend with people will be beneficial for our work, whether the experience is positive or negative.

In Matt. 4:23, we see Jesus among the people. He is there again in Matt. 9:35. How often did a multitude gather to him? Jesus was the ideal preacher and is the ideal preacher's model. For Jesus, it was about people. May we humbly follow his lead!

3

the preacher & discouragement
jacob hawk

Your feeble key turns the rusty lock of an all-too-familiar ghost town: the Monday morning church building. As you walk through the foyer, you bundle the bulletins abandoned in the auditorium. You pour out the crusted coffee cups sitting on the counter. You place the used, tarnished hymnals and Bibles back into their racks in the pews. These items prove that, just a few hours ago, there was life in this place. There was laughter in the halls. Discussion in the classrooms. Communion with the Lord.

But today, things are different. This is Monday, the nemesis of its predecessor, Sunday. The summit of Sunday's shine has descended into the valley of Monday's blues. This is the subtle, yet surreal reminder that you must now work up the courage, energy, and ability to do it all over again.

It's exhausting to even think about it. In 144 hours, additional sermons, classes, and articles will be demanded from the ink of your pen and wrinkles of your mind. The foyer of fellowship has diminished into the den of decay, and for one reason—

The preacher's discouragement.

So now, as you reminisce about yesterday and dwell on today, you find yourself staring deep in to the mirage of Monday morning, asking, "What will I say?" When the summit of Sunday comes in six sunrises and sunsets, what message of the Lord will I bring?

You know the routine. After you conquer Monday, the week progresses. You survive the meetings, sermon preparation, counseling, and other ministerial demands. But all these distractions lead you back to "Discouragement Drive," a road no minister wants to travel, yet one every minister ventures down.

Now it's Saturday evening. Bulletins have been re-printed with new information, ready to be read and crumpled. The coffee grounds are waiting to be liquefied. The hymnals and Bible are ready to be turned by tornado-like hands of the young and old. Everything and everyone is ready, except you, the preacher. Not because the sermons aren't ready—they are. Your class is complete. The bulletin article has been edited at least twenty times.

But you're not ready. Your mind is distracted; your heart is heavy. Monday morning's question, "What will I say?" has evolved into Saturday evening's question: "How will I say it?" Will I be dynamic or static? Will I come across emotional or superficial? Will people turn their ears to the message or turn their gears to Cracker Barrel? Will I be effective? On Saturday evening, when your head should hit the pillow with excitement and satisfaction, it grazes the sheets with anxiousness and discouragement.

Nevertheless, the cycle continues, and you travel through the roller coaster of Sunday. Adrenaline rushes and hushes. The classes are taught and the sermons are preached. As people exit the auditorium, they might even say, "Great job, preacher!" Or, "You really touched me today!" Or, "That stepped on my toes!"

The cliché compliments and comments have been voiced, but you still return home Sunday evening with questions and concerns.

Monday morning, you asked, "What will I say?" Saturday evening, you wondered, "How will I say it?" But then, as Sunday wanes, the most discouraging question surfaces on schedule in your mind: "Why can't I say it better? Why can't I be more like the preacher down the street with a larger congregation? Why can't my jokes be funnier, my illustrations clearer, my applications truer, my insights deeper? Is this really what I should be doing with my life?"

Yes, it is. Without a doubt, you have chosen the right profession. God is pleased. But here's the problem: Satan masterfully works his way into your palace of passion and demotes it to a hut of heartache, and you, only you, are affected by his schemes.

Preachers today aren't the only ones bearing the battle scars of discouragement. Remember Elijah in 1 Kings 19? When our fingers flip through the pages of the inspired text, and when we arrive at the scene, Elijah, one of God's greatest servants, is as burned out as a marshmallow tucked into a s'more. He had completely surrendered his life to God's will. He had walked on the soil of Mount Carmel and faced the mighty prophets of Baal. He had challenged them to a prophetic duel and won! When the prophet of Baal baptized his altar with fierce torrents of H2O, through faith, Elijah lifted his head to the heavens, asked for fire, and it came as soon as the request left his lips. Not only did it drop from the sky like a feather; it consumed everything. The people couldn't help themselves; the response was natural. "The Lord is God."

He was. He is. He always will be.

But after this life-changing, faith-strengthening episode, Elijah disappeared into the den of discouragement. After her prophets puppets were destroyed, Queen Jezebel searched for Elijah with a vengeance. She even placed a bounty on Elijah's life, asking for his head on a silver platter. Understandably, Elijah ran like an Olympian at the starter's pistol. His life was at stake. The God who provided Elijah's life seemed to forget about his very existence. We've all been there.

Let me suggest some practical ways to avoid discouragement.

Surround yourself with other preachers. When I began my ministry, I preached for a small church in the Texas Hill Country. We were the only Church of Christ in town, and the surrounding towns had only one Church of Christ as well. Each congregation was at least thirty miles away. This made it very difficult to find that camaraderie my heart was seeking. The preachers within a ninety-mile radius would meet once a month for a lunch and period of study. However, I never attended these meetings because of the time and expense of travel. Looking back, that was one of the biggest mistakes I made in my first few years of preaching. I felt alone because in many ways, I was. Others were reaching out to me, but I wasn't reaching out to them.

As I moved to a bigger town and a bigger church, I discovered more opportunities for relationships with fellow preachers. Today, even through social media, we can know what's happening in each other's ministries. This was a huge blessing for my ministry, and it will be for yours also. I could discuss my struggles and listen to the struggles others were facing. We shared sermon ideas, confessed sins, and prayed for each other's life, ministry, marriages, and children. We helped equip each other to faithfully serve the King of kings.

If you feel discouraged in your ministry, find other ministers in your area. I guarantee that they feel discouraged from time to time as well. They haven't faced a challenge you haven't faced, and vice versa. They can probably shed some light for you or gain knowledge from you. You don't have to be a lone man stranded on an island. You are swimming in a sea of preachers who want to help you. Don't make Elijah's mistake—don't convince yourself that you're the only one left. God reminded Elijah that 7,000 warriors were still holding high the name of Yahweh. Today, I don't know the exact number of preachers who are lifting up the cross of Christ, but this I do know—it's more than one. It's more than you or me. Find them.

Seek periods of refreshment. This might sound elementary, but we must define "refreshment" correctly. Some things we view as "refreshing," but they may not be. When I mention periods of refreshment, I'm not just talking about time with your family, although that is crucially important. Many ministers make the mistake of forgetting that Jesus is married to the church, not them. Consequently, they lose their families in the process.

When I mention periods of refreshment, I'm not talking about personal times of study, although these periods are refreshing. I'm not talking about vacation time or how much sleep you get every night. When I mention periods of refreshment, I'm highlighting seminars, lectureships, and gatherings where your soul is refreshed and your preaching strengthened. From encampments in the mountains to assemblies at universities, something can be found for everyone.

Preachers, when you reach an agreement with your elders about your annual time away, distinguish the difference between personal vacation and personal development. Your family needs you to spend a vacation with them so memories can be made as a family. But you need time for personal development so your ministry can be centered more on Jesus. As powerful as it is to find camaraderie with a few preachers, it's equally important to find camaraderie with all brethren. Not only will you reconnect with those you know, and build connections with those you don't, but you will also hear great preaching and teaching from great men of God. You will gain new insights. You will develop new ideas for your congregation. And most importantly, God will be glorified through the process. This is a blessing you don't want to miss.

Saturate yourself in study, and let nothing compromise that period of growth. Personal study is key to successful preaching. Notice that I specified the ministry of preaching. Different ministries require different levels of study and academic discipline. Nevertheless, if you have been charged by God and hired by men to be a voice and teacher of a congregation, your life must be adequately and proportionately consumed by study. Nothing, absolutely nothing, can compromise that period of growth.

> Practice these things, immerse yourself in them, so that all may see your progress. Keep a close watch on yourself and on the teaching. Persist in this, for by so doing you will save both yourself and your hearers.
>
> 1 Tim. 4:15–16

This passage is one of the most pertinent and powerful reminders for preachers in all the Pastoral Epistles. It's a humble reminder that ministry without diligence is ministry without deity. Ministry without discipline is ministry without direction. Study is the glue that fits the pieces together.

The timing of these words in Paul's first letter to the young preacher Timothy is crucial. Throughout the letter thus far, Paul had touched on matters of training for godliness, placing hope in Jesus rather than in the world, and devotion to sound preaching and teaching. But here, in these words of wisdom,

Paul strokes the paintbrush gently across the canvas of the preacher's mission.

The preaching life is a process. As preachers begin their preaching, they realize the job requires shoulders strong enough to carry the burden, that people won't always be impressed by their sermons, nor will they always agree with the positions they support. A preacher soon learns that a congregation may not believe he's as talented, dynamic, or intelligent as he believes himself to be.

One afternoon, a preacher and his wife were riding home from Sunday services. The preacher was becoming quite confident in his preaching. He was mastering the art of picturesque illustrations, new applications, and purposeful humor. As they were riding along, he looked at his wife and asked, "Honey, just how many great preachers do you think there are in the world?" She replied," One less than you do." A congregation's cough medicine of humility can be pretty strong, but a preacher's wife's potion is even stronger! If you need to stay grounded, your wife will gladly aid the process!

But Paul reminds us that we shouldn't worry about our preaching being a process—in fact, that's how it's supposed to be. That's why he says, "Take pains with these things; be absorbed in them so that your progress will be evident to all." Yet progress isn't attainable without study. Reading and reflecting on *the* Book provides the progress our ministry requires.

In addition to progress, Paul mentions the importance of sound doctrine in the preacher's preaching. Someone once asked me, "Are you a preacher, or a gospel preacher?" I asked them, "Is there a difference?" A preacher who doesn't preach the gospel isn't a preacher, just a speaker. The church doesn't need gentle orators, but bold proclaimers. Granted, bold preaching shouldn't be defined by one's ability to break barriers of sound.

Yelling, screaming, and condemning don't produce the results desired by God. Gospel preaching isn't defined by the number of verses you quote or the length of time you preach.

The preaching needed in Christ's church is powered by passion, conviction, and distinction. It's preaching that elevates the name of Jesus. It's preaching that tells the old story in new ways. It's preaching that makes us better, stronger, and purer. It's preaching that doesn't try to impress or depress. It's preaching that keeps it simple but doesn't simplify the profound truths of Jesus to cotton candy fluff. It's preaching that values New Testament restoration.

This preaching doesn't just happen. It requires study. I remember in my undergraduate studies at Harding University, our homiletics professor, Dr. Philip Thompson, made a powerful (yet humorous!) point about a preacher's misunderstanding of sermon preparation. Dr. Thompson said, "Many times, preachers will sit by the creek and lay under the stars, waiting for the inspiration of the Spirit, and then get up to preach and say, 'The Spirit placed this message on my heart.' Boys, don't blame the Spirit for something that bad. Certainly the Paraclete, the Comforter and Guide, can do much better than that." As God's mouthpiece, we speak on his behalf, but God doesn't speak for us. We surrender our hearts, minds, and existence to his will, yet he charges us to adequately prepare to make his will known.

The last segment of this passage is one that rattles my bones and chills my spine. It paints the picture even clearer as to why James says, "Not many of you should become teachers, my brothers, for you know that we who teach will be judged with greater strictness" (Jas. 3:1). Paul tells Timothy that the congregation's souls are in his hands. Granted, God—not the preacher—will be the judge. It is the Word that pricks hearts, not the wordsmith. The Holy Spirit will educate more than the lecturer standing behind the lectern. But nevertheless, Paul reminds a preacher beginning his journey in preaching, "You better be careful; what you preach will not only save you, but also those who listen to what you say."

How many congregations have wondered into the abyss of apostasy because of the preacher? How many congregations have devalued the pattern for the church because of a minister who wanted to change things that must not change? How many churches are weaker because of the weak understanding of God's will coming forth from the spokesman? Preachers carry a tremendous responsibility that can only be borne through the grace, mercy, and power of God. But it is a responsibility that can only be accepted through devotion to study and of showing yourself approved.

March 4, 1881 was a beautiful spring day in Washington D.C. James Garfield stood on the Capitol steps, placed a hand on the Bible, another on his heart, faced a crowd of thousands, and was sworn in as the 20th President of the United States. Like every Inauguration, it was a day ripe with patriotism, pride, and power.

After the ceremony was over, a curious listener came up to James Garfield and asked, "Mr. President, what does it feel like to have the most honorable job in the world?" Garfield shook his head and said, "Sir, to be honest with you, I feel like I've been demoted." The man was confused and asked, "But Mr. President, what do you mean? You're the most powerful man on the face of the earth. You're the commander-in-chief of the United States of America. How in the world have you been demoted?" Garfield responded, "Sir, before I became the President, I was a gospel preacher, and there is nothing more honorable than that." When the 20th President of the United States grabbed the presidential anvil, he felt like he had stepped down.

There is nothing more honorable than being a preacher for the church that belongs to Jesus. Is it discouraging at times? Yes. Can it be disheartening? Of course. Difficult, scary, and even heartbreaking at times? Absolutely. But we don't quit. We don't back down. We carry the cross of Christ, and we preach every sermon like it's our last. We have the greatest job in the world, and a crown of life is waiting for each of us if we remain faithful to our duty. "How beautiful are the feet of those who preach the good news!"

4

the preacher & stress
jay lockhart

Have you noticed that, during Jesus' ministry, he never seemed to have been in a hurry? Here was the Son of God who was on the greatest mission in history, who had limited time in which to fulfill it, yet he never seemed to be in a hurry! True, he was often with the multitudes, but he would sometimes take the time to go with one person who needed him. How different my ministry is! I seem to always be in a hurry and never quite finish all I think needs to be done. The result is that I am often stressed out, anxious, and frustrated.

Why was Jesus so different? He did not seem to be frustrated, anxious, or stressed out. Here is the answer: Jesus always did right then what needed to be done most. If I could learn to do this, my stress level would decrease immediately. In this chapter we want to look at what stress is, what the causes are, and how we as preachers can overcome too much stress in our lives.

Webster's defines stress as a word from the Latin term *strictus*, meaning *distress*, and is "mental or physical tension or strain" or the "urgency, pressure...causing this." The stress factor is the gap between the demands made upon us and our apparent strength to meet those demands. Stress is not always a bad thing. We are equipped by our Creator with mechanisms that help us to perform tasks, get things done, and achieve goals. However, too much stress is harmful, leading to frustration and anxiety that can cause us to become ineffective in our work. Stress can also affect our health. A sign in a doctor's office read, "Hyper-tension (too much stress) can affect your heart, arteries, brain, and eyes." We need to be aware of the harmful effects of stress, seek to understand its causes, and try to discover what we can do to reduce harmful stress.

a case study

In 1 Kings 19:1–18, God's prophet, Elijah, was experiencing stress. During the reign of wicked King Ahab, Elijah had just won a great victory at Mount Carmel over the false prophets of Baal and had slain them. When Ahab told his wife (the equally evil Jezebel) what Elijah had done, she sent a message to the prophet saying, "So may the gods do to me and more also, if I do not make your life as the life of one of them by this time tomorrow" (1 Kings 19:2). Elijah became afraid and ran for his life to the wilderness near Beersheba. He was stressed. What were his symptoms?

1. He depreciated his work since he wished to die (19:4).

2. He underrated his work since he felt what he had done did not matter (19:10a).

3. He exaggerated his problems by saying, "I, even I only, am left, and they seek my life, to take it away" (19:10b). While Elijah was dealing with a crazy queen and an evil king, he was not taking

into account the fact that the God who was with him at Mount Carmel was with him in his dealing with Ahab and Jezebel, so he exaggerated the problem.

4. He gave up on his dreams since he believed he was the only one left who was faithful to God, and he was no better than anyone before him (19:4b, 10b).

Elijah did four things as he dealt with the stress created by Jezebel's threats.

1. Elijah rested and fed his body (19:5–8). Unless one feels well through receiving the proper amount of rest (this includes time away from one's job) and eating a healthy diet, he will likely struggle with stress.

2. Elijah released his frustrations (19:10). God does not mind if we complain to him (consider the Psalms of David in which he expresses frustration). However, our frustrations and complaints must always bring us back to our faith that is expressed in believing that God is, in trust that accepts his promises, and in obedience to his will.

3. Elijah refocused upon God (19:11–14). He came to see that God can accomplish great things through one small insignificant man.

4. Elijah returned to his work (19:15ff) with renewed strength and vigor. He realized that there is time enough to do what needs to be done most and, with God's help, he was able to deal with his stress.

the twin sister

The twin sister of stress is anxiety. When one is experiencing unhealthy stress, he begins to worry. He worries because there does not seem to be enough time to get everything done that needs to be done. He worries because he fears he will fail. He worries about others being disappointed in him. As he worries, stress is increased. Notice three things about worry:

1. Worry is irreverent. It fails to recognize that God is still on his throne and works in the lives of his children (cf. Rom. 8:28).

2. Worry is irresponsible. It wastes energy and burdens us so that we cannot be engaged in constructive and creative problem solving.

3. Worry is irrelevant. It cannot change anything. It has been estimated that 50% of the things we worry about never happen, that 30% are about the past which we cannot change, that 12% are too petty to affect the future, and that just 8% legitimately deserve our concern.

Notice three principles from Phil. 3 for dealing with worry.

1. Make everything a matter of prayer. Paul said, "Do not be anxious about anything, but in everything by prayer and supplication with thanksgiving let your requests be made known to God" (Phil. 4:6). It is easy to fall into the trap of thinking that we will handle the "little things" by ourselves and "bother" God with only the "big things." But we should remember that with God, nothing is too small or too big—God is interested in whatever troubles us. Therefore, rather than worry about anything, let us pray, "and the peace of God, which surpasses all understanding, will guard your hearts and your minds in Christ Jesus" (Phil. 4:7).

2. Point your thoughts in the right direction (Phil. 4:8). When we think the right kind of thoughts, we will begin to be governed by our faith instead of our feelings. We are then in a position to say, "Today, I will be thankful that I am alive, and that God is with me and will work in my life. Today, I will grow as a Christian should, I will become what God intends for me to become, and I will be what I am supposed to be."

3. Take actions against your worries. In closing his thoughts to the Philippians, Paul stated, "What you have learned and received and heard and seen in me—practice these things, and the God of peace will be with you" (Phil. 4:9). If you are worrying over a problem you can do something about, do it! If you are worrying over a problem you can do nothing about, turn it over to God and move on.

Before leaving these thoughts on anxiety, let us consider three things Jesus taught his disciples to do to prevent worry.

1. Place your trust in God when you face issues beyond your control. Consider the birds of the air (your Father feeds them, and you have more value than they do); consider your height or the length of your life (you cannot increase either of these through worry); consider your clothing (God clothes the lilies, and the grass and he will clothe you) (cf. Matt. 6:25–32).

2. Put God first (Matt. 6:33) and you will be happier, healthier, and more content.

3. Take life as it comes, one day at a time (Matt. 6:34). Plan for the future but live well today. You cannot bear today all the possible problems (real

and imagined) that the future may or may not bring. Remember that God intends for his people to live the abundant life (John 10:10).

causes of stress in the preacher

While others may face some of the same stresses that preacher's do, there are some causes of stress that are related to the preacher and his work.

Moving to a new location. Taking a new job always causes stress for the preacher and his family. The preacher's wife experiences stress as she leaves old friends and comfortable surroundings to begin again in a new house, a new church, a new community, and a search for new friends. The preacher's children experience stress as they leave friends and must adjust to a new school and new surroundings in a new place. The stress endured by his family adds to the preacher's stress that he himself experiences because of the move. Even though there is excitement in a new work, it is difficult for the preacher to begin preaching for a different church, serving under new elders, and to adjust to his new situation. When I was a young preacher, it was not uncommon for a preacher to move every two or three years. In those days, if a preacher stayed at one place for five years, he had stayed for a long time. I am thankful that we have moved beyond the preacher staying for such a short time with a church, and that both preachers and elders have seen the value of longer ministries. It is quite common now for preachers to stay at one place for ten, fifteen, twenty, or more years.

How can a preacher build a lasting ministry with one church and avoid the stress of moving? First, let him continue to be a diligent student of Scripture. Nothing can take the place of study if the preacher wants to continue his work in one place. I once heard of a preacher who had two hundred sermons, and when he preached all of them, he moved and preached the same sermons at another church before he moved on to still another church. Obviously, the preacher preaches the same sermons over and over again throughout his ministry, but he must never preach a sermon again without thoroughly re-studying the text, his points, his illustrations, and his application. In a word, remain fresh in your presentations through diligent study.

Second, in establishing a long stay with a church, the preacher should also choose his battles carefully. Every issue that arises in ministry is not worth "going to the mat" for. Of course, there may be doctrinal issues, and when these arise, our appeal must always be to Scripture. However, many issues are not of a doctrinal nature, and when these arise we must be tolerant, easy to be entreated, and willing to get along. Good advice would be to seek peace and be sure to work for unity in the church. The preacher should not insist on having his own way, and he should have respect for others in all matters of opinion. He should respect the elders and support them in public and private, in word and in deed. He should avoid conflict when it is possible, and longevity in his ministry will be enhanced.

Finally, the preacher should be involved in the lives of the people. He should be there for them when they are in the hospital, when they experience death in their families, when babies are born, when their children marry, and when they enter the straits of life. When beginning a new work, he can try, in the first year if possible, to visit in the homes of all the members. He can seek to bond with as many of his people as he can. These things will be appreciated by the members of the congregation and will bring stability for a longer ministry with one church.

However, there does come a time for a preacher to move on to a new work. Before he decides to move, he should consider that if he moves because of problems where he is, he will have a different set of problems where he is going. We are imperfect people who work with imperfect people, and every church has its problems. A preacher needs to think long and hard before he decides to move, knowing that a move will bring stress to him and his family.

Meeting deadlines. There are a number of deadlines that a preacher must meet. He normally will have at least two sermons and two classes to prepare each week, as well as articles to write, and other speaking engagements for which he must prepare. In addition to my weekly sermons, classes, and bulletin articles, I write regularly for various brotherhood publications and speak at gospel meetings, lectureships, and civic and school organizations. As I write this chapter, I am trying to meet a deadline for this assignment. Additionally, we have deadlines for participating in funerals, weddings, and various other responsibilities that come with our involvement in the work of an active and growing congregation. These deadlines increase our stress levels. What can we do to deal with this stress?

The first thing I would suggest is to plan ahead. The preacher needs to know where he is going with his sermons. He should plan his preaching well in advance, for a quarter or even a year. If he knows where he is going, he can always adjust his preaching plan, but by planning ahead, he will relieve his stress levels. It helps me to preach in series. I often present a series of four to eight (or more) sermons on a given theme. Each lesson stands on its own so as not to bog down either myself or the church, but I do tie the messages together. I preach through books of the Bible. The advantage of doing this is that I not only know where I am going, but I also am forced to preach on themes that come up in the book which I might not otherwise cover. Planned preaching helps release stress. Additionally, I keep a file of "possibilities" for future funerals, bulletin articles, gospel meetings, and civic talks. By doing this, I avoid the additional stress of having to decide at the last minute what I will use under various circumstances.

Balance between work and family. If the preacher has a wife and children, his stress levels will increase as he tries to give proper time to his work and avoid neglecting his family. My wife and I have a "date night" each week when possible, usually on Friday nights. If something interferes with Friday, we will often plan another night. When our children were young, we did not have a "family night." We tried that, but it became "an appointment with dad," so we tried giving our children some time when we did not have it to give. I did not want my children to resent my work because I did not have time for them. I attended their games, their band concerts, and other school activities. I wanted to be there for them, and I often adjusted my schedule to do it. I did not want to be so busy helping others that I neglected my own. I sometimes had to say no to others in order to say yes to my family. My family appreciated this decision, and I believe the church appreciated it as well. I did not make a big deal of it, and there were times when I had to say no to my family, but I tried to avoid the stress that would naturally come if I neglected them.

Helping troubled families. Most preachers I know, including myself, are not trained counselors, but we certainly do a lot of it. When families are in trouble, they usually turn to the preacher for help. This causes an increased level of stress. We want to help when and where we can, but we often feel very inadequate. Here is a word of advice: do what you can to help troubled people—pray with them, share biblical principles with them, and share advice with them from your experience and understanding. But recognize your limitations, and do not hesitate to refer them to professional counselors with whom you become personally acquainted and know they will give advice from a Christian perspective. Helping troubled families is stressful, and the preacher should do what he can. But if he knows his limitations, stress will be held to a manageable level.

Control anger and be willing to forgive. The preacher may be mistreated by someone in the church. This treatment may produce resentment and lead to anger and stress. He may justifiably believe this person is wrong. But he should try to avoid a disposition of anger and get over it (Eph. 4:26, 31). He should have an attitude of forgiveness, whether or not the person involved asks for forgiveness. Unless he does this, the person he feels has wronged him will control his life. Every time he sees this person or thinks of him, he will be resentful, and stress will increase. Preachers must forgive others and move on. If he does not develop a spirit of forgiveness, the person he feels has wronged him will cause him to be dissatisfied in his ministry, and the end result could mean he will end up moving.

final thoughts

As preachers deal with stress, let them remember these things:

Prioritize time. At the beginning of the week, he should make a list of what he will do. Make a list of what must be done and list those things in order of importance. This will decrease stress.

Take some time off. Through the years, I have kept office hours. People need to know their preachers are "on the job." Of course, the nature of his work will mean he will be in and out of the office during the day, but people need to know he is there. I recommend a day off each week for a change of pace that will help prevent "burn out." In my own experience, I have found a day off does not work well for me. I am in my office Monday through Friday. Saturday is a day to accomplish things around my house (yard work, washing my car, catching up on "honey-do's") during the morning, and study for Sundays on Saturday afternoons and evenings. Rather than a day off for me, I prefer to occasionally take an afternoon for golf or a day or two for a short trip out of town for relaxation, and I have never had a problem with elders or a congregation concerning this arrangement. It may be different in various situations, but the preacher does need some time off because it releases stress.

Learn how to say "no." A preacher cannot do everything, he cannot be every place, and he cannot be involved in every activity. The church will survive, even if he is absent. So he should prioritize his time and learn to say, "No."

Recognize the preacher's primary work is preaching. The preacher should never approach the hour of preaching unprepared because he was involved too much in other activities during the week. He should prepare, prepare, and prepare for the delivery of his sermons. He should set deadlines during the week for when he wishes to have his research done, when he wants his sermons outlined, complete with illustrations and application, and when he wants to be ready to preach. Then he should stick to his plan. Will there be interruptions? Of course. Will there be times when his schedule is in shambles? Yes. Will there be times when he is better prepared than at other times? Probably. However, he needs to have a plan and should try to stick with it.

Consider elders to be friends. The preacher should talk often with his elders and share with them his hopes, dreams, and vision for the church. He should share with them his views concerning his work, family, and philosophy for preaching. He should make them his friends so that when he attends an elders' meeting, he is not fearful and filled with stress. If the preacher is invited to an elders' meeting, and is considered an adversary by the elders, or considers himself to be an adversary, it is little wonder that such meetings produce stress. Therefore, let preachers build friendships with elders, and he will diminish fear and decrease stress.

These things have helped me in dealing with my stress. Do I experience stress? Oh, yes, but it is manageable. It is my prayer that these suggestions will help other preachers manage their stress as well.

5

the preacher & criticism
jeff a. jenkins

No one really likes criticism, but it seems to be a part of everyone's life, including preachers. We should be careful that we don't think preachers receive more criticism than anyone else, but preachers know we receive our fair share!

What is criticism? Dictionary.com defines it as "the act of passing judgment as to the merits of anything." It is also defined as the "art of analyzing and evaluating or judging the quality of a literary or artistic work, musical performance, art exhibit, dramatic production, etc." The work of ministry and the task of preaching certainly falls under this definition. Every aspect of ministry, including the delivery of sermons, is subject to criticism. The question is not, "Will we be criticized?" but, "How will we respond to criticism?"

When we think of criticism from a biblical perspective, a few passages come to mind. In Exod. 17:4, Moses asked the Lord, "What shall I do with this people? They are almost ready to stone me." The context of this question was the constant complaining of the people of God to Moses. Every preacher who has poured his life into preaching and ministry understands exactly what Moses was feeling as he said these words. We have heard God's people complain about our sermons' length (too long/short), content (not enough Scripture, not practical enough), or delivery (not enough passion, too theatrical, too much humor, etc.). James Kennedy said, "Of course, I don't suppose there has ever been a preacher who escaped his share of the barbs of criticism."

Someone once quipped:

- If he preaches sound doctrinal sermons, he ought to be more interested in everyday problems of people. If he focuses on practical life-situations, it's because he doesn't know much theology.

- If he emphasizes the importance of giving, he has his mind on money. If he doesn't stress regular giving, he is a poor steward of church finances.

- If he is especially strong on soul-winning, he should be more concerned about community and national affairs. If he is active in social and political betterment, he ought to concentrate on evangelism.

- If he tries to encourage a friendly atmosphere in the congregation, he is not conducting a dignified service. If he places a priority on reverence and order during worship, he is giving the church a reputation for being stuffy and unfriendly.

- If he makes a point of conveying basic spiritual truths that he may be all things to all people, he tends to be vague and too general. If he addresses specific sins within the congregation, he has quit preaching and gone to meddling.

Some of you reading these words have heard these exact criticisms, or at least some form of them. It might help us to remember that great men of God have always been criticized for their work or teaching.

Another example of a man of God receiving criticism was the great leader Nehemiah. Notice the barrage of criticism he faced:

> Now when Sanballat heard that we were building the wall, he was angry and greatly enraged, and he jeered at the Jews. And he said in the presence of his brothers and of the army of Samaria, "What are these feeble Jews doing? Will they restore it for themselves? Will they sacrifice? Will they finish up in a day? Will they revive the stones out of the heaps of rubbish, and burned ones at that?" Tobiah the Ammonite was beside him, and he said, "Yes, what they are building—if a fox goes up on it he will break down their stone wall!"
>
> Neh. 4:1–3

Wow! They criticized God's leader at every turn!

We are also reminded of the apostle Paul. After he discussed the external pressures, persecutions, and problems he had to deal with, he added, "And, apart from other things, there is the daily pressure on me of my anxiety for all the churches" (2 Cor. 11:28). There is no doubt that included in the daily pressure was the criticism he received from false teachers and brethren who attempted to undermine his ministry.

We must remember the prophecy concerning what would happen to our Savior when he came into the world. "He was despised and rejected by men; a man of sorrows, and acquainted with grief; and as one from whom men hide their faces he was despised, and we esteemed him not" (Isa. 53:3). The writer of the book of Hebrews taught that remembering Jesus could help us when we face trials of our own. "Consider him who endured from sinners such hostility against himself, so that you may not grow weary or fainthearted" (Heb. 12:3).

If the Savior, the perfect preacher, received criticism from those who heard him preach and those who knew of his work, we should not find it unusual that we will also face criticism. He said to those of us who follow him, "If the world hates you, know that it has hated me before it hated you. If you were of the world, the world would love you as its own; but because you are not of the world, but I chose you out of the world, therefore the world hates you" (John 15:18–19).

We live with the realization that everyone who accomplishes anything worthwhile will face criticism. It doesn't happen just to preachers. It happens to anyone trying to do something good for others. It happens to all Christians involved in working for and living for the Lord. We should be careful that we don't develop the Elijah Complex:

> So Ahab sent to all the people of Israel and gathered the prophets together at Mount Carmel. And Elijah came near to all the people and said, "How long will you go limping between two different opinions? If the LORD is God, follow him; but if Baal, then follow him." And the people did not answer him a word. Then Elijah said to the people, "I, even I only, am left a prophet of the LORD, but Baal's prophets are 450 men."
>
> 1 Kings 18:20–22

Some people seem to have been born to be critical, or they think that they have the gift of criticism as if it is a spiritual gift.

They seem to think their purpose in life is to sit around and be critical of others. Again, the issue isn't if criticism will occur—it is how will we handle it when it comes our way?

listen

James, the brother of our Lord, said, "Know this, my beloved brothers: let every person be quick to hear, slow to speak, slow to anger" (Jas. 1:19). It has been correctly stated that God gave us two ears and one mouth; we should thus listen twice as much as we speak.

The problem with listening to criticism is that it can sometimes be hurtful. Because of that, we tend not to want to listen. The truth is that we should be thankful for criticism. If it is good criticism, it will help us make corrections and grow. It can make us better preachers, Christians, family leaders, and men.

We need to consider the possibility that we are not always right. "Whoever conceals his transgressions will not prosper, but he who confesses and forsakes them will obtain mercy" (Prov. 28:13). Since no one is perfect, we should listen to what others have to say. "Like a gold ring or an ornament of gold is a wise reprover to a listening ear" (Prov. 25:12).

If it is bad or incorrect criticism, it will help us to become more humble—more like Jesus. We will learn who and what we need to pray about. It will help us become more sympathetic to those around us.

learn

There are two kinds of criticism. One is called "constructive." It is designed, in the critic's mind, to bring a positive end. Sometimes, we deserve criticism and it can be helpful. However, constructive criticism can be as painful to the one being criticized as that which is called "destructive." Both hurt.

Criticism can drag you down. As we mentioned earlier, Moses found this out. He didn't want to be a leader. He knew he would have to pay the price of criticism. In the final analysis, Moses agreed to lead this band of slaves. Their lot in Egypt had been bad. Their children had been massacred; cruel taskmasters had oppressed them. One would think that Moses would have been praised for his leadership, but he was not. The story of the wilderness journey is one in which Moses is constantly maligned. One would think the people would appreciate his courageous leadership, but they cried out: "Would that we had died by the hand of the LORD in the land of Egypt, when we sat by the meat pots and ate bread to the full, for you have brought us out into this wilderness to kill this whole assembly with hunger" (Exod. 16:3).

God provided for their needs. He gave promise of a future. Again, they complained, criticizing Moses. The reason? He had run out of water again, and once again, they murmured against him, complaining that he had led them out of Egypt. What had been so horrible before looked so good in a difficult moment. Broken by criticism, Moses fell on his face before God and cried out, "What shall I do with this people? They are almost ready to stone me" (Exod. 17:4). We, like Moses, have been the recipients of devastating analysis.

What can we learn from criticism? We can learn something about ourselves. We can learn where we need to grow in our walk with God. We can learn more about humility. We should do everything possible to develop the humility of Christ.

> Have this mind among yourselves, which is yours in Christ Jesus, who, though he was in the form of God, did not count equality with God

THE PREACHER & CRITICISM

> a thing to be grasped, but emptied himself, by taking the form of a servant, being born in the likeness of men. And being found in human form, he humbled himself by becoming obedient to the point of death, even death on a cross.
>
> Phil. 2:5–8

We can also learn something about others when they criticize us. Many times, someone hurt or wronged by someone else can't help but criticize. Our goal should be to look past the pain that is in someone's heart and see if we can find something useful in their criticism. Often times, people who are ultra-critical have received a lot of criticism themselves. Maybe they received a lot of criticism from their parents when they were young. Maybe it came from peers or teachers in school as they were growing up.

We should ask God to help us have the wisdom to learn from those who are critical. The brother of our Lord said, "If any of you lacks wisdom, let him ask God, who gives generously to all without reproach, and it will be given him" (Jas. 1:5). Our God will supply us with the wisdom and strength to learn from any criticism that comes our way.

leave

Criticism often involves petty concerns that don't matter. We need to have the discernment to distinguish between criticism that is helpful and not helpful, and to leave invalid criticism alone. This is where we need trusted advisors and confidantes to help us. We don't need just "yes" men around us to only say what they think we want to hear. Rather, we need close friends who know us well, who will be honest with us, and who will tell us if the criticism is valid. It might be our wife, another family member, another close preaching friend, an elder, or another church member who we trust to be honest with us. G. K. Chesterton observed, "There are no words to express the incredible abyss between complete isolation and having one person who loves you on your side. We may concede to the mathematician that two times two is four. But two together is not simply two times one; where two are together, two is two thousand times one."

let

We should let criticism remind us to be careful about being critical ourselves. If you have ever been criticized, you know how it can hurt. You understand how criticism can affect your work, how it can keep you up at night, and how it can affect your mental as well as your physical health. When we receive criticism, it should cause us to ask, "Am I guilty of criticizing others?" When we are hurt or feel wronged by others, it's easy to lash out at others. But Jesus said, "So whatever you wish that others would do to you, do also to them" (Matt. 7:12). The apostle Paul reminded us, "Let no corrupting talk come out of your mouths, but only such as is good for building up, as fits the occasion, that it may give grace to those who hear" (Eph. 4:29).

lean

We need to lean on the Lord to help us. Ultimately, our goal in life is to please the Lord.

> For am I now seeking the approval of man, or of God? Or am I trying to please man? If I were still trying to please man, I would not be a servant of Christ.
>
> Gal. 1:10

> But with me it is a very small thing that I should
> be judged by you or by any human court. In fact,
> I do not even judge myself.
>
> 1 Cor. 4:3

To accomplish this goal, we must have God's help. We are not wise enough to do this by ourselves. The wise man said, "Trust in the LORD with all your heart, and do not lean on your own understanding. In all your ways acknowledge him, and he will make straight your paths" (Prov. 3:5–6).

We must not allow criticism to keep us from focusing on the work we are doing for God. We have a mission. We are to proclaim the Good News to those who desperately need to hear it. We are to be about the work of ministry. "As for you, always be sober-minded, endure suffering, do the work of an evangelist, fulfill your ministry" (2 Tim. 4:5). Our focus in life is to bring glory to God in everything we do (1 Cor. 10:31).

Leaning on the Lord will also lead us to pray for our critics. It is difficult to be angry at someone or to want to lash out at them if we are praying for them. There is something about praying for those who have wronged us that will change us. "Love your enemies and pray for those who persecute you, so that you may be sons of your Father who is in heaven" (Matt. 5:44–45). It is possible that our kindness will lead our critics to change their ways.

If you are a preacher, you will be criticized and corrected. It's coming. We must prepare for it and realize that God can use it to make us better preachers, better men, and better Christians. How we respond to criticism, both from friends and enemies, is absolutely critical. I think about the times in my life when I haven't responded humbly to correction. I pray that God will forgive me for those times and help me grow in the way I respond to criticism. I pray the same for all men who endeavor to proclaim the unsearchable riches of Christ.

6

the preacher & his family
adam faughn

If a preacher is truly involved in ministry, it can't be denied that the work has a great deal of stress associated with it. Those who preach accept that, and as we continue in the work, we understand it more and more strongly. Too often, however, those whom we love the most—our families—bear the brunt of that stress through no fault of their own.

From the outset of this chapter, let me say that a preacher does not have to be married or have children in order to fill the role. I am friends with several preachers who are single, and they are doing a great job in the vineyard of the Lord. In fact, sometimes a single man is better equipped to face certain situations due simply to the freedom of being unmarried. Paul, of course, exemplified this and wrote about it for all Christians in 1 Cor. 7. It would do elders well to prayerfully consider these passage before they release to the brotherhood that they are looking for a "married man with children" as their next minister.

That said, the majority of preachers are married, and most will have children also. Being the leader in the home is hard enough, but when you have the stresses of ministry constantly on your mind as well, the responsibility becomes great. In this chapter, we will discuss ways a preacher should lead his home in a way that pleases God.

focus on christ's example

No doubt, every preacher who has been in the pulpit more than a few months has presented a sermon about the home, and he has been sure to mention Eph. 5. We shower our audience with insight into the God-given roles for husbands and wives in the home, and we point out the perfect pattern laid out in that text—the relationship between Christ and his church. The question we must all answer, though, is this: Does that pattern describe my home?

Sometimes, we know the information intellectually from the text, but we struggle to live it out in our own lives. Those of us who spend hours pouring over Scripture should know as well as anyone the perfect example of Jesus Christ. He was the ultimate servant-leader who was willing to sacrifice. "For even the Son of Man came not to be served but to serve, and to give his life as a ransom for many" (Mark 10:45). Of course, Paul wrote that Christ "gave himself up" for the church (Eph. 5:25), and he did so through the shedding of his blood (Acts 20:28).

Preachers, does that picture describe your home? Does your wife see you put her first? Are you sacrificial towards her so that she knows that she is of supreme importance in your life? Would she answer the same way?

Few, if any, reading these words will be called upon to literally die in the place of their spouse. To be honest, that is rare. However, we can still do certain things to show our wives that we are sacrificing for her, and some of those things must involve our ministry.

Preachers who are always building their lives around the needs of other families and the wants of other people will have a very difficult time showing their wife and children that they are truly the priority. We all understand that there are times when we must run out of the house due to an emergency. Those times will happen, but every phone call or text message should not take us away from our family. Sometimes, the words "I'll be there later," or even, "No," are necessary.

May I remind all of us that we did not marry our ministry? You said "I do" to a lovely woman, not to a career! If you have officiated at a wedding, you have reminded the couple that they are taking their vows, not only in the presence of the people assembled there, but also in the presence of God. We need to remember that we did the same. We vowed before the God of heaven to love and serve our wife through anything in this life. We probably uttered the words, "Forsaking all others." That phrase does not exclusively apply to the sexual relationship in marriage. I must be truly intimate with my wife, and that includes making her the highest human priority, with my children immediately after. My career, as noble as it is, must come down the list, and at times, it needs to be "forsaken" in order to show my wife that she is my partner and priority.

being the "pastor"

Preachers in the churches of Christ spend a lot of time explaining to others that we are not "the pastor." Where we preach is not "our" church in the sense that we are not "over it." Ultimately, Christ himself rules the local congregation (Eph. 4:15), but elders are to oversee the work (e.g. Phil. 1:1). We are members of the congregation, but we are supposed to preach and teach under the oversight of the elders.

At home, however, we are in some ways the "pastor" of the little congregation that resides there. The qualities that we preach when it is time to appoint new shepherds over the congregation should be cultivated and clearly seen in our homes.

In the same way that God has elders over a congregation (Acts 20:28), he has placed you as the head of your family. Your attention and focus should be for the benefit of your wife and children. How other families conduct their traditions and the ins-an-outs of daily living may help you do a better job, but your focus is on those who are sleeping under the roof with you each night. Keep your eyes and your mind on your family!

Also, take a long and prayerful look at those qualifications of elders that you have preached so often. Do they describe you? Do they describe you when you are at home? One of the most difficult things for preachers to overcome is to be "preacher-y" when they are at the church building, and anything but that when at home. Both are wrong! We need to be faithful, no matter where we might be. After all, that is what God requires.

Think of what you desire in your eldership, and that will help you decide what you need to be in your home. We want elders to be serious, yet approachable. We want pastors who know us well and have our best interest at heart. We want our shepherds to protect us from the enemy of our soul. We desire Bible-based wisdom and insight. Further, we like to get to know these men and see that they have a personality that includes both the serious and the fun.

If you consider those things, do you see that your family desires the same from you as the leader in your house? While Scripture never states that fathers are the "pastor" of the home, we can see that the roles are similar, and the same things required of pastors in the Lord's church are needed by men in their homes.

let her be herself

Some preachers try to make their wife conform to a "preacher's wife model" that they conjure up. Often, the wife of a preacher is the person in the congregation who feels the most pressure to uphold an "image" no one can really define.

Unless your wife is doing something contrary to God's will, you should let your wife's personality shine through. You married her for a reason, but many husbands allow a congregation to determine what personality his wife will have. As a real man, you should protect your wife's personality and let her be herself.

For some, that may mean that the wife is not involved in every ministry or event the congregation has. I firmly believe the preacher and his wife should be heavily involved, but if there is a ministry she has no interest in, let that go. If she does not want to teach every quarter in the Bible school program, then talk to the elders of the educational director on her behalf. Make it clear that your wife is more than willing to teach, but she deserves quarters away just like any other teacher deserves.

Some preachers fail to ask important questions in the interview process concerning the role of his wife. Elders and search committees can say, "She'll be a member just like everyone else." But what do they mean by that practically? As a husband, you should ask specific questions. Will she be required to teach a certain age or grade, and will she ever get time off from teaching? Will people criticize her if she goes to visit her family a couple of times each year, or do they consider it truly healthy that she still be connected to her family? Is there a ministry, class, or activity that the preacher's wife is assumed to head up? These questions, and similar ones, need to be addressed in a very comprehensive manner to determine not only if the preacher's personality fits with the congregation, but also if his wife's will also.

as for those pk's

The old joke is that preachers' kids would be OK, except they spend too much time with the elders' grandkids. While that might bring a smile to a lot of faces, it doesn't to mine. For one thing, I am a PK (i.e. "preacher's kid"), and being a preacher, I do not want my children to feel as if they are totally different from other children in the congregation.

Instead of addressing you as "preacher," let me address you for a moment as "dad." Dad, why do you want your children to act a certain way? Maybe you are a bit stricter when it comes to entertainment choices, or maybe you are a stronger disciplinarian than other dads. While being strict is not necessarily a bad thing, and disciplining your children is certainly biblical (cf. Prov. 23:13–15; Heb. 12:11), we must ask why we are that way. Honestly evaluate yourself in light of this question: are you stricter because you want your children to be godly, or are you strict because you want to keep your job? For some preachers, the answer might not be what they want to admit.

We know "the verse" addressed to fathers, and it is one verse that I often wish were not in the Bible. At the very least, I wish it were worded differently, so as to clearly address both the mother and the father—and if I had my way, it would be addressed solely to moms! Of course, I speak of Eph. 6:4—"Fathers, do not provoke your children to anger, but bring them up in the discipline and instruction of the Lord." Preachers, we need to remember that there is not an addendum to this verse giving us permission to take discipline to an extreme level.

It is very easy to focus on the phrase, "discipline and instruction" and fail to see and practice the other phrases. The first is "Do not provoke (i.e. "exasperate," NIV) your children to anger." While that phrase is generally applied, I want to make a specific application, and I pray I am not stretching the text too far. We must be careful that we do not make our children angry that we are in ministry by the way we treat them. Part of the discipline and instruction we must give to our children is a healthy balance of life. We must spend both quality and quantity time with our children, and that does not always mean we are going to another gospel meeting as a family or visiting another widow. There is certainly a place for helping our children grow in their appreciation for using their time to the glory of God, but they also need to see that there is time as a family doing various types of things. If all they ever experience is another "church thing," they will be angry and exasperated; they will feel that the church is taking daddy away from them, or is at least monopolizing their time together.

The final phrase is easy to miss: "of the Lord." Brothers, we must be careful that we do not focus on our own glory or on having the "model family" so that others will think we are something special. Instead, we should be striving to show our children holiness and how to use their special talents and gifts in the service of the King. We should not desire that our children be good just so that we keep our job or so our kids have a certain PK look (whatever that is). Instead, we should want them to be good in order to honor God through their unique gifts in whatever circumstances they might face. That will include taking time to go to Vacation Bible School and gospel meetings, and it will include visiting nursing homes and sending cards to shut-ins. But we should not do those things just because we are the preacher's family (and we should never present it as such); we should do those things to build into our children a desire to serve God in any way they possibly can.

If your son does not desire to be a preacher, that is quite all right. He might have a greater impact on the Kingdom as a doctor or teacher or coach than you have had. If your daughter comes home with a man one day, and he is not planning on being a preacher, that is OK. She is not rejecting you. She may have found the next medical missionary, or they may build wealth to help dozens of students attend Christian colleges. Raise your children to follow their own specific bent, or as Solomon put it, "In the way he should go," not in the way you *think* he should go (cf. Prov. 22:6), and focus with great intensity on the outcome. The outcome is not that your son desires to be a preacher or your daughter marry a preacher, but that they are faithful to the Lord and impact their world for him, using their own unique talents.

practical "to do's"

Every person is different, and each family has its own dynamic, but there are certain things that need to be true in every home. These may seem random, but these suggestions are practical things that will help you lead your family. By the way, I am in no way perfect at following this list, so it is my prayer that we will seek to grow in these areas:

Take your vacation time to actually vacation. Too many preachers take their families on a "vacation" while daddy holds a(nother) gospel meeting. It might be great to take the family on a mission trip or vacation from time to time, but you need to get away as a family and just relax or go visit relatives.

Let them see you laugh. Life is serious, and trying to help souls get to heaven could not be any more serious. But not every moment in life is serious! Your children need to see you laugh at times when life is just funny. It will not only help you with health, since laughter is good medicine (Prov. 17:22), but it will also help your children see the balance that needs to be had in life.

Have family devotionals. These do not have to be hour-long expositions of difficult biblical texts. Simply help your children sing their favorite songs, memorize some verses, or learn to talk biblically about subjects they are facing. What better memory could you give your children than regular time with the family, meeting together to worship God?

Seek outside help when necessary. Preachers are not above the need for marital counseling or help as a dad. Since we often do counseling, even if informal, we can begin to believe that we are above the need for counseling ourselves. As you have likely told others, though, your marriage is certainly worth the extra effort and seeking help when you are struggling.

Date your wife. She needs to see you in "non-preacher" mode, and she needs to see you in those romantic settings that you enjoyed before you married. Go out to eat, even if you can't afford fancy places. Take walks in the park or ride bikes through the neighborhood. Go on a picnic or have a night out at a hotel, even if it is just across town. Pick up her favorite candy bar or brand of coffee on the way home "just because." Let her know with your actions that you are still pursuing her above every other woman in the world, and even above your job. As an added tip, put your dates on your calendar so that, if someone calls and wants to meet, you can say, "I already have something scheduled for that time. Let's meet another time."

Pray for your family. I think—at least I hope—that most of us pray with our family. Maybe we take a moment regularly before a meal, or we pray before our children go to bed. But are you spending time in prayer for your family? How long has it been since you took the names of your wife and children before God? How specific are your prayers on their behalf? We preach often that prayer really works. Do we show that in our own lives as leaders of the household?

Try to stay. What I mean is, try to stay in the same place while your children are growing up. There are obviously situations in which it is better to move, but constant moving is difficult on the family, especially the children. It may mean some added stress on you, but it could also mean added stability that your children seriously need. If you decide to move, make sure you communicate to your children a positive attitude and an appreciation for both the congregation and the community where you have been. While it may be difficult in the moment, follow the Golden Rule in how you speak about the place you are leaving.

leadership is hard

Consider for a moment that you are required by the Lord to lead your home. It is an awesome and, at times, overwhelming responsibility. As a minister, you are a leader, but you are in most cases under the oversight of an eldership. In the home, however, you are the head of the household, and there is no human authority higher than you. You answer to the God of heaven and have the goal of showing his example daily. The demands of being a godly leader in the home can take their toll.

You must admit that leading is hard and be willing to face that difficulty with humility. It is amazing to me how many great men of God we read about in the Bible struggled mightily when it came to their home life and leadership. David stands as a pillar of Scripture, yet his house was racked with difficulty. In many ways, his home wrote the definition of "dysfunction." Solomon was wise beyond his years and could lead a nation unlike few before or since. He could not, however, lead his home properly, and it ruined the kingdom's destiny. Eli was a priest who was quite influential among God's people, but his boys were ruinous and destroyed themselves.

These accounts, along with many others, provide a striking reality for us. First, they are obviously cautionary tales. We are reading about great leaders, both secular and religious, who lost control of their homes. Too many preachers help lead others to Christ through the rough terrain of the Christian journey, but they don't take the time and energy necessary to lead their own families. Noah may not have had a perfect family, but I hold him in high regard. After all, at least he got his own family on the ark! When our lives are over, if the same can be said about us, we have been successful leaders.

The accounts of men like David and Eli also teach us something else, however. David had a wreck of a home, yet he was still a man of whom God said, "I have found in David the son of Jesse a man after my heart, who will do all my will" (Acts 13:22). Maybe you have not been leading your home as you should. It fills you with guilt and remorse on a constant basis. Brother, remember that God is gracious. Today, you must begin leading in a godly way. If you have been exasperating your children, pray for wisdom in how to show them the proper balance of life. If you have been distant from your wife, pick up a bouquet of flowers on the way home and take her out on that "next first date."

Even if your children are grown and gone, you can write a letter to them or make a phone call. It may be difficult, but your leadership in taking the initial step will speak volumes about your heart. If your reasoning in doing these things is to honor God, his grace will help you.

I took a long day in an attempt to finally complete the first draft of this chapter. I had started and stopped several times, so I decided to take one day to work on almost nothing other than these words. After I had been working solely on this chapter for an hour or so, my wife called. I set the work aside to talk with her. She and my children were getting ready to visit family for a day or two. I'm glad they are making that trip because she loves her family, but I always miss her and the kids when we are apart.

As we spoke, I had to make a confession. I do not recall my exact words, but they were something like this: "It's been hard today. Here I am, writing a chapter about the preacher and his family, and you are all leaving to go on a trip. What makes it a lot harder, though, is that I know I'm not everything I am writing."

Brothers, this chapter was not written by an expert, but by someone with a passion to help families. I have no doubt that every preacher reading these words has a desire to help people. Maybe you have more of a passion for the homeless or for mentoring younger men. Whatever your area of emphasis, we as preachers love to help people. We have a desire to see as many people as possible enjoy God's blessings in this life and to live with him eternally. We thus spend our lives seeking opportunities to help. That's why I agreed to write this chapter!

I must make an appeal, however, and it is an appeal that is first made to me as I peck away at the keyboard. Who in this world do I most desire to help? If I said "I do" to that sweet lady to whom God led me, then it needs to be her. And if the Lord blessed us with a bouncing baby boy or a precious treasure of a girl, then they are next on the list. It does not matter if you stand before a dozen people on Sunday morning or thousands; your primary desire in life needs to be for your little family to live for God daily and share the bliss of heaven. My appeal is that we live each day with that engrained in our hearts, delivered through our words, and shown in our actions.

7

the preacher & his finances

dale jenkins

Kerry and Jill were on fire for the Lord. Fresh out of school with their newly minted B.A. in Bible, they were married the same month and came back from their honeymoon to begin their first work at the Oak Street Church of Christ in a small southern town. They couldn't have been more excited. They were going to change the world—or at least convert everyone in their little town.

The first two years were stellar! He was loved and she was adored, as much by the congregation as by each other. The church grew spiritually, in energy and in numbers (attendance and contribution). Of course they had their bumps in the road. Some thought he focused on numbers too much; others believed his sermons were not as deep as they had had in the past. With the numbers going up, some felt reverence in the assembly suffered. There were a few older folks who felt things had changed. There was a sermon or two where he'd taken a risk, and it hadn't worked. But all that was fine.

Life was good.

Sometime about the middle of year two, Jill found out she was pregnant. Nothing shocking there—they were ready for kids. And the church was as happy as he was. Nothing is more fun than a new preacher's baby! As the New Year rolled around, he thought, with the contribution up about 30%, and with them expecting their first child, he would get some sort of raise. He wasn't in it for the money, but everybody in the church just assumed his salary was going up as other things did. And with a child on the way and money already tight, they knew what he made and how much he worked.

But the raise never came. Kerry wasn't bitter, mad, or even upset. After all, there were more missionaries being supported and more activities to be funded. They could make it. But he was a tad disappointed.

Baby Hayden couldn't have been cuter. He was the youth group's unofficial mascot and the pride of every older lady in the church. His little face just beamed when his dad would take him from his mom's arms to go "shake the congregation out" after the service. Kerry also beamed with appropriate pride.

Of course with a new baby, there were new expenses. Their insurance, which they supplied on their own, had gone up. There was formula and diapers and clothes for a growing little boy.

When year four began and there was no raise, Kerry felt jilted. He'd heard of this sort of thing before: that some leaders believe a preacher maxes out at a certain salary. He sort of understood. But Jill was just mad. She knew how seriously Kerry took his work and how much time he devoted to his sermons and ministry. She could see the numbers on the board as clearly as anyone.

Money became tight. Sadly, Kerry and Jill began living paycheck to paycheck. Their savings were just about gone. There had been a couple of overdrafts with their subsequent fees when checks beat their way back to the bank before their paycheck had cleared. One had been sent back to a local market, and the phone call was embarrassing. Her college clothes were showing serious wear, and his didn't fit right. The stress had caused him to add a few unwanted pounds.

That wasn't all. Kerry felt like others knew he was struggling, and it affected his confidence in the pulpit. Everything was going great, but he was collapsing on the inside. Did they really even want him anymore? Maybe not giving a raise was their way of saying his work wasn't "up to snuff." Add to that the fact that the bigger church on the other side of the county had offered him their pulpit when it opened and a good bit more money. But he didn't feel right about it. He loved these people, was committed to them, and thought it felt wrong to move just for more money.

Jill didn't demand, but sure came close to it, that he talk to his elders about a raise. He did, and then he wished he hadn't. He felt both dirty and used. One elder seemed to understand but didn't say a lot. Another said, "If a young man can't make it on what we pay you, he isn't worth shooting. When I was your age, I didn't make half what we pay you." Another said that they would see what they could do. He left the meeting at the point of tears. In fact, riding home that night alone, he shed a few as he prayed to handle all they'd said with the right spirit. He wanted to be humble, but he felt he was worth more. He wondered if perhaps he should have never gone into preaching at all. He felt like a failure as a husband, father, provider, and preacher. Most of all, he dreaded telling Jill. She would hit the roof. And he knew that tomorrow, more of those ugly overdraft notices would hit his mailbox.

What happened? Where did Kerry go wrong? What should he have he done differently? What can he do now?

A dear friend who is not a preacher wrote this to me a couple of years ago:

Preachers are notoriously bad money managers.
Some of that comes from the traditionally small
paychecks they have received. However, even as
salaries have risen in larger churches, preachers
still file bankruptcy at alarming rates. And worse
still is the plight of preachers as they reach ages
that render them unable to continue in their
ministry. They have no retirement. You remember
when preachers opted out of Social Security in
droves in the 1970s and '80s. Some of this stems
from a real desire to 'seek first...," but often it is
a lack of training and resources. They have very
little to save, and often what they do have is spent
on keeping old cars running and even old church
vans running as well. Churches and elderships,
sadly, feel very little responsibility to encourage
young preachers to save or manage their finances
in any way. I know of a few horror stories where
preachers were forced to retire and then just
cut loose to live at or below the poverty level
on their spouse's social security, a few speaking
engagements, and part-time janitorial work!

My friend is right, but I believe what I've often heard about
our brotherhood: "Our brethren will do better when they know
better."

One of my best young preacher friends ran into a very well-
known preacher at Chick-fil-A a few years ago. He had a coupon
to pay for his lunch. The older guy said, "Chicken and money—
two things preachers like." I've never met a minister who got into
ministry for the money, but as George Bailey told Clarence in *It's
a Wonderful Life* when Clarence said, "We don't use money in
heaven,"—"It comes in pretty handy down here, bud."

No, we don't do this for the money, but we nonetheless have

a biblical responsibility toward our families (1 Tim. 5:8) and a duty to work (2 Thess. 3:10). While we must avoid the love of money (1 Tim. 6:10), those we work with have a responsibility too (1 Cor. 9:10). It seems most of us have had little training concerning a preacher and his finances, so many end up in trouble at some point. This is a subject that is very needed.

Some time ago on TheJenkinsInstitute.com, our Featured Writers offered insight on the subject of preachers and money. With thanks to those experienced writers, I want to glean some of the best of the best of their thoughts (as well as a few of my own) to give collective advice of hundreds of years of study and personal experience.

Here are ten tips for ministers and their money:

1. *It is wrong to love money, but it is not wrong to make money.* Having a lot or a little money is neither good nor bad. If you preach, it is not wrong to move over matters involving money. What is wrong is to not support your family. In 1 Tim. 5–6, Paul deals with money matters. Widows who should receive support (5:9–16), elders who are to be paid (5:17–18), the love of money (6:10), and the proper use of money (6:17–19). He begins that section with something every sacrificing preacher should note: "But if anyone does not provide for his own, and especially for those of his household, he has denied the faith and is worse than an unbeliever" (5:8). No, you are not sinning and should not feel guilty if you need to move or want to move for money considerations. But if you do not take care of your family, you *are* sinning. And friend, make sure your wife is aware and on board, or you will find yourself without a ministry or a family. You can have both, but Scripture requires that if you have both, you must pay attention carefully to both.

2. *Learn to negotiate.* Greed is a sinful, ugly thing. But we also need to be aware that we are involved in two worlds when moving. One that is highly spiritual in the sense of our work, responsibility, and weighty matters involving souls, the feeding of them, and things eternal. The other involves the fact that a church is involved in a business matter of coming to terms on paying a preacher. The fact is simple for most preachers: Times have been better for the last few years. As we work toward helping churches realize a laborer is worthy of his hire, we must never forget the tremendous sacrifices of those who have gone before us. We can feel greedy, but let us not become greedy. Beginning a new work is the best time to work toward an agreement that will be one that can help you be free to do your best work. Don't be greedy, but ask for things that will make your work go more smoothly (e.g. materials/book allowance, retirement account, travel allowance, paid personal growth programs, technology budget). I ask that the leadership at least commit to discussing my salary each year with the intent to at least provide a cost-of-living increase. Jerrie Barber has often said that if there is not a cost-of-living raise, then a preacher is worth less than the year before. Elders may say "No," but these are things that might help you. I would caution strongly against accepting a role that will put you where you can't pay your bills, or you will be unhappy with the pay. But regardless, if you accept a job at a salary, don't spend your time bellyaching about how little they pay you. You agreed to that salary. My friend Ronnie says preachers shouldn't "poor mouth" about their pay.

   3. Learn from past mistakes. "For the righteous falls seven times and rises again, but the wicked stumble in times of calamity" (Prov. 24:16). If I understand this verse correctly, it is saying that I'll make mistakes as I live for God, and I should learn from them. But the person not living for God doesn't learn from his mistakes. When you are passing through a difficult time, write down lessons you are learning. This will both help you to process your own emotions, as well as possibly help you to avoid repeating those patterns. I keep a file called "moving" and write down what I would try to do differently the next move. Whether it be in coming to an agreement on money or sermons I'd preach, this file has been very helpful to me.

4. *Live on a budget.* As Dave Ramsey says, "If you don't know where your money is going, you will wonder where it went." Without a budget, it does not matter how much you make; you will spend it all and be broke. While the text is referring to our stewardship of God's truths, 1 Cor. 4:2 also applies to our stewardship of God's monetary riches. "Moreover, it is required of stewards that they be found faithful." In most marriages, one spouse will be a saver and the other a spender. But for this to work, both must give a little. The spender must be willing to tighten up, and the saver to loosen up. You must have a mutually prepared and agreed upon spending plan. It should include giving, spending, and saving. I encourage you to revise it often and to sometimes break it, but to at least have one and discuss it monthly. Don't fight over money all the time; it's not worth it. A Gallop survey a couple of years ago said the number one thing couples argue over is money. Let's not be like everyone else. I would add here to do your best to avoid debt—"Owe no one anything, except to love each other, for the one who loves another has fulfilled the law" (Rom. 13:8).

5. *Don't forget to do good works.* I love Heb. 13:16, "Do not neglect to do good and to share what you have, for such sacrifices are pleasing to God." We must not forget that we are God's work of art, that we were created to be involved in good works (Eph. 2:10). Paul told Timothy to instruct the rich to be rich in good works (1 Tim. 6:18). We are rich in our country, and we were not blessed to increase our comfort, but to bless others. The older we get and the richer we get, the more easily we distance ourselves and our memories from times when we did not have much, or from those who do not have much. I believe our *first* and *best* gift must go to the local church (1 Cor. 16:1–2), and this is true regardless of our emotions about that congregation. If not, we will always find excuses not to give, and as my dad used to say, "attempt to 'elder' our own money."

But I would also encourage preachers to make it possible that, when needs arise, they can be a part of alleviating those needs. One of the purposes of work is defined in part of Eph. 4:28, "that he may have something to share with anyone in need." When a disaster happens, you can't just ask for others to help, but you can participate and lead in helping. Do the little things: Stick a $100 bill in the Bible of a family you know is struggling with money issues. Send a contribution to a work you believe in. In so doing, you also fulfill the instruction of Heb. 10:24, to "consider how to stir up one another to love and good works." But you can only do all of this consistently if you follow rule #4. Don't forget to do good works!

6. When it comes to money issues, avoid carrying that weight to the pulpit with you. I wrote this to a dear friend recently who was depressed over money matters: "I know that getting rid of that pressure has to be a huge relief. Nothing frustrates me and brings me down quite like money problems. That is when I feel most helpless and hopeless…" When we struggle with money issues, it is like a weight that we carry around our necks. In the pulpit, it affects our confidence, focus, and may even affect our feelings toward our leaders (e.g. "If they paid me better, things would be better…"). As ministers, we can become needy and feel we need to be ministered to, thereby short-circuiting our ability to minister to hurting people. We can become bitter about our pay, and that comes across in anger in the pulpit. We can become embarrassed about our financial situation, and that will sap the energy and confidence from our preaching. Few things can affect your preaching more negatively than money issues.

7. Avoid the misnomer that more money cures everything. Most Americans tend to believe that if we just had a little more money, it would make life better. Paul would counter this with, "In any and every circumstance, I have learned the secret of facing plenty and hunger, abundance and need. I can do all things through him who strengthens me" (Phil. 4:12–13). Most of the extremely wealthy people I know talk about how much they enjoyed life when they didn't have anything but each other. What is better than money is learning the lesson of how to handle the money you have. The Lord said you cannot serve both God and money. If you grow to love money, you will grow to hate God. If your money is on your mind all the time, you will end up serving it. You can live on a lot less than you have or make. Life will be better, not with more, but when you learn to live with less. I advise young preachers to find a banker who is a trusted brother, someone they can meet with for advice and talk to before making major decisions. If they are a part of the congregation, that's an added bonus for your leaders—they will probably appreciate your attempt at accountability. Also, learn from and lean on older, wiser preachers. Share your struggles with them. Learn to realize that no one understands preachers like other preachers. Find guys from whom you can learn and with whom you can grow.

8. Remember what you do will affect the next preacher. Yes, you can help or harm your influence by how you handle your possessions, but you will also affect others. Sadly, preachers in general have a bad reputation with banks over how they handle money. This is often not because of dishonesty, but because they have not been paid well enough to take care of matters and get in trouble as a result of a lack of training. But if you mishandle money, the next guy will suffer because of it. His influence will be diminished even before he gets there, and doors might be closed for evangelism. His influence in the church and with the leaders will also be affected. I worked at one place where I was not given a church credit card because a previous guy had abused it. One more item in this area would be to consider the needs of the person who follows you. If God has blessed you where you do not need much, do not handicap the next guy by keeping the salary low by turning down raises to the point that the elders feel the next guy should not be paid much, or that they put themselves in a situation where they can't pay as much.

9. Consider the future. While we are to live in the present, we also live in three time zones. As we preach and teach the grace, goodness, and justice of God, we preach to help people deal with their past so that they can live for God in the present and with him in the future. So in your personal finances, be as responsible for your future as possible so that the church will not have to suffer by your lack of oversight, and your family will not have to fear. Try to build up three-months salary in savings. Begin now setting something aside each month for retirement, even if you never plan to retire. It will serve your family well when something happens to you.

10. Trust God! In this case, #10 is really #1. All of our dealings with "earthly mammon" are a test of our trust in God. I know it gets hard to see your way out of situations. At times, it becomes bleak, and you feel weak, but I can assure you with David: "I have been young, and now am old, yet I have not seen the righteous forsaken or his children begging for bread" (Psa. 37:25). I know Matt. 7:11 is true: "If you then, who are evil, know how to give good gifts to your children, how much more will your Father who is in heaven give good things to those who ask him!" The Father cares for you, and it will all work out. Your mission is to trust him, to be faithful to him, and to strive to be his servant.

I want to close with a quote a dear friend shared with me years ago that I hope will stay as close to the front of your vortex as it has mine: "For every discipline learned, there are many rewards." Kerry and Jill? They made it just fine.

Remember this, and you will too: "Trust in the LORD with all your heart, and do not lean on your own understanding. In all your ways acknowledge him, and he will make straight your path" (Prov. 3:5–6).

8

the preacher & sin
kirk brothers

I like westerns. I have read Louis L'Amour books for years. I enjoy old cowboy movies featuring the likes of Audie Murphy, John Wayne, and Jimmy Stewart. One of my favorite John Wayne movies is *Hondo*, a story written by Louis L'Amour. There is a fight at the end of the movie in which Hondo (John Wayne) is with a small outfit of soldiers who are attacked by Indians. John Wayne kills the Indian chief, Silva, and the Indians retreat. Several old westerns depicted battles as ending when the chief was killed in battle. The Indians would call off their attack because the tribe concluded it was "bad medicine." Though I don't agree with the Hollywood stereotype of Indians, I believe this scene illustrates one of Satan's favorite modes of attack: going after the leaders.

satan's attacks

Every once in a while, Scripture gives us a glimpse into the eternal realm. The first two chapters of Job represent one of those glimpses. The narrator of the Job story allows us to listen in on a conversation that Job and his friends seemingly never know about. It shows us the true nature of the devil. It depicts him living up to his name, Satan, the adversary.

Can you imagine what it would be like to have God brag on you? Every leader for God should live such that God could. God bragged on Job in the presence of Satan. We see the Adversary's attitude in his response, "Does Job fear God for no reason? Have you not put a hedge around him and his house and all that he has, on every side? You have blessed the work of his hands, and his possessions have increased in the land. But stretch out your hand and touch all that he has, and he will curse you to your face" (Job 1:9–11). The story that followed was one of great pain and enduring faith. It serves as evidence that Satan attacks the leaders.

Jesus knew these attacks as well. Both Matt. 4 and Luke 4 tell us that Jesus was confronted by Satan. While the Savior was still in the afterglow of his baptism and the Father speaking from heaven, three mighty blows rained down upon him. The Messiah fought back with integrity and drove his adversary away. Still, the devil merely "departed from him until an opportune time" (Luke 4:13). Satan is relentless.

Satan later went after Jesus' followers. In Luke 22:31–32, Jesus says, "Simon, Simon, behold, Satan demanded to have you, that he might sift you like wheat, but I have prayed for you that your faith may not fail. And when you have turned again, strengthen your brothers." Though Jesus shifted to the singular when he said, "I have prayed for you" (i.e., Peter), Jesus used the plural form when he said, "Satan has demanded permission to sift you." Satan was after all of the apostles, though Peter would feel his wrath in particular.

Satan is a persistent foe. In his classic work, *Between Two Worlds*, John R. W. Stott tells of the famous English preacher, Hugh Latimer. One of Latimer's best-known sermons is "The

Sermon of the Plough." In this lesson, Latimer stressed that the devil was the hardest working preacher in England. "There was never such a preacher in England as he."[1] I am reminded of one of my father's favorite sayings: "It is a war out there, and the devil never takes a day off." Scripture is filled with examples of Satan's efforts. It is also filled examples of leaders who succumbed to temptation and sin. King David defeated the great giant, Goliath, but fell before the giant of lust (2 Sam. 12). Barnabas succumbed to peer pressure and practiced favoritism and hypocrisy (Gal. 2:13). Demas loved the world more than the Lord (2 Tim. 4:10). The trail of fallen leaders continues. If you will give me a moment, I need to step away for a bit to prove my point. I'll be right back…

OK, I'm back. Here is what I found while I was away:

- School officials in Ohio were indicted in connection with a rape case.
- A star college athlete was under investigation in another rape case.
- A Pennsylvania detective was suspended for possibly covering up murders.
- A mayor of a large city admitted to smoking crack cocaine.

I briefly stepped away from writing this chapter and went to a national news website. In less than ten minutes, I found the four articles listed above. These articles offer evidence that Satan continues to tempt, and leaders continue to tumble.

One could add stories of youth minsters who acted inappropriately with church secretaries, elders who embezzled

---

1. John R. W. Stott, *Between Two Worlds: The Challenge of Preaching Today* (Grand Rapids: Eerdmans, 1982), 27.

money, and preachers who split churches. Paul said that all "have sinned and fall short of the glory of God" (Rom. 3:23). This, of course, includes preachers, youth ministers, and leaders among God's people. The point of the first half of this chapter is not only that God's leaders are capable of sin, but they also have been the special objects of Satan's attacks. Do not assume it cannot happen to you. Pride and naivety go before the fall.

the savior's answer

What are we going to do about these attacks? There was a period of about 3½ to 4 years when I boxed for exercise. I had no desire to box professionally. It is a very dangerous sport, and I was not very good at it. I did, however, often spar with professional boxers, including three fighters who have fought on ESPN. I was one of the human punching bags that helped them get ready for their fights. I am right-handed, but on a few occasions I had to swap to fighting left-handed and leading with my right-hand jab. I did this when the person I was sparring with was going to fight a southpaw. Each fighter is different, and boxers must learn to adapt to their opponent.

Temptation can come to the preacher in many forms, and we must adjust to each. John stated, "Do not love the world or the things in the world. If anyone loves the world, the love of the Father is not in him. For all that is in the world—the desires of the flesh and the desires of the eyes and pride of life—is not from the Father but is from the world" (1 John 2:15–16). Notice the apostle's three-fold division of loving the world: lust of the flesh, lust of the eyes, and the pride of life. The temptation of Eve consisted of these three elements:

- Lust of the flesh — "Good for food"

- Lust of the eyes — "Pleasing to the eye"
- Pride of life – "Be like God" (cf. Gen. 3)

The temptation of Jesus also reflected the same three renditions of temptation:

- Lust of the flesh — "Turn stones to bread"
- Lust of the eyes — "Look at the kingdoms"
- Pride of life — "Throw yourself down" (cf. Luke 4)

Sin will often come to the preacher in the same ways:

- Lust of the flesh — Temptation to have inappropriate relationships with members of the opposite sex, or to love money and gain it dishonestly.
- Lust of the eyes — Watching Internet pornography.
- Pride of life — Enjoying the praise of people and sacrificing our principles and the truth to be liked by people.

How can we counter these temptations and attacks? Jesus may be able to give us some insight into this. He prayed in the garden of Gethsemane while surrounded by men who did not understand the gravity of the situation. Judas and a cohort of soldiers were just moments away. Jesus wanted a few precious moments alone with the Father before facing the cross. He wanted his friends to watch for the approaching army while he prayed. Yet he also wanted them to watch spiritually as well. His words to the apostles may serve well to assist us as we face temptation: "Watch and pray that you may not enter into temptation" (Matt. 26:41). Luke 21:36 states, "But stay awake at all times, praying that you may have strength to escape all these things that are going to take place, and to stand before the Son of Man."

The apostle Paul was also in the habit of putting the concepts of watching and praying together in his teaching.

> Praying at all times in the Spirit, with all prayer and supplication. To that end keep alert with all perseverance, making supplication for all the saints.
>
> Eph. 6:18

> Continue steadfastly in prayer, being watchful in it with thanksgiving.
>
> Col. 4:2

Let us explore how alertness and prayer can assist us in fighting against sin.

watch

The apostle Peter said, "Be sober-minded; be watchful. Your adversary the devil prowls around like a roaring lion, seeking someone to devour" (1 Pet. 5:8). Imagine that you have just learned that a lion has escaped from a local zoo and has been seen in your neighborhood. How would you act when you left your house? Would you walk nonchalantly to your car without a second glance? Would you calmly mow your yard without a care in the world? My guess is that your answer to each of these questions would be, "No!" You would be constantly watching for the lion so he could not catch you by surprise. It must be the same with Satan.

Paul understood the value of watchfulness. Consider the following examples from his message to the elders at Ephesus and his letters to the churches at Corinth and Thessalonica:

> Therefore be alert, remembering that for three years I did not cease night or day to admonish every one with tears.
>
> > Acts 20:31
>
> Be watchful, stand firm in the faith, act like men, be strong.
>
> > 1 Cor. 16:13
>
> So then let us not sleep, as others do, but let us keep awake and be sober.
>
> > 1 Thess. 5:6

Paul also noted the value of alertness in Eph. 6:18. This comes at the end of his discussion of the armor of God. It is appropriate to end such a discussion with a reference to alertness. Soldiers who were not alert or who slept on duty could lose their lives. How do we as preachers avoid the temptation to sin? We watch for Satan's attacks. What does this watching look like?

Acknowledging our weaknesses. Watching for Satan starts with knowing our personal weaknesses. Each of us has specific things that tempt us. What tempts one person may have no impact on others. We need to be honest with ourselves about our temptations and struggles with sin. With one preacher, the temptation may revolve around money. For another, it may be pornography. A third minister may struggle with lying to make himself look good. Our wives are often more perceptive than we are in recognizing these danger areas. We would do well to heed their advice.

Friendly fire is a common danger in military conflict. Confederate General Stonewall Jackson was wounded on May 2, 1862 due to friendly fire and died a little over a week later. Lt.

Gen. Leslie J. McNair, head of Army ground forces, was killed by friendly fire at Normandy on July 25, 1944. Friendly fire injuries and deaths result when soldiers are unclear as to who the enemy is, and they mistake friend for foe. Alertness to sin involves knowing what our personal demons are (the enemy) so that we can more easily avoid them.

Avoiding the temptation situation. Once we have considered what tempts us most, we can then better avoid the situations that motivate us to do wrong. God told Joshua and the children of Israel to completely remove the pagan nations from Canaan when they took possession of the Promised Land (cf. Josh. 10:40). They failed to do so. They left many pockets of Canaanites behind (cf. Josh. 15:63, 16:10, 17:13). These pagan nations would be thorns in the side of God's people for years to come. It should not surprise us that Israel struggled with idol worship when we note that idol-worshipping peoples were allowed to remain among them.

Preachers should watch the influences they allow around themselves. We need to avoid situations that might lead to sin. If we struggle with pornography, we need to make sure that our computer viewing is done in a public place (such as in our living rooms, rather than our bedrooms), and that we put guardian programs on our computers. We need to avoid being alone with women other than our wives. We should establish very clear ground rules in counseling situations. We must be careful in how we hug women (e.g. no direct chest-to-chest hugs). Using an accountant can help us keep our taxes above board. Simply put, we need to avoid circumstances that might lead to sin.

Accessing accountability. We are accustomed to people depending on us. We don't want to appear weak, so we try to do things on our own. The reality is that we need help like anyone else. God wanted the Christian life to be a shared existence.

This is embodied in the term *koinania*, "fellowship," that is found in places like Acts 2:42. Paul stated, "Bear one another's burdens, and so fulfill the law of Christ" (Gal. 6:2). Don't be afraid to ask for help. If any of us broke a leg, we would go to the doctor. We wouldn't try to set it ourselves. Why is it that we will not ask for help when we are struggling with a particular sin? If an addiction has been going on for a while, we are likely going to need professional counseling to help us overcome it. Often, we just need an accountability partner. This is someone we trust who can serve as a mentor, hold us accountable, and pray for us. Remember the words of James, "Therefore, confess your sins to one another and pray for one another, that you may be healed. The prayer of a righteous person has great power as it is working" (Jas. 5:16). A Christian mentor or accountability partner can help us be aware of our actions and weaknesses. They allow us to see ourselves from the outside. This needs to be a person we know who loves us and loves the Lord. Knowing that there is someone who will keep our confidences, yet lovingly confront our actions and attitudes, can make all the difference in our efforts to watch for sin.

pray

Jesus not only asked his apostles to watch; he also asked them to pray. The West Tennessee Cardiovascular Center has an interesting advertisement about what to do if you have a heart attack. Their slogan is "Survive, Don't Drive." The commercial encourages people to call 911 when they sense the symptoms of a heart attack, rather than trying to drive themselves to the hospital. When heart-attack victims drive, they are a danger to others, and medical personnel cannot help them. Victims are better off to call and wait for the professionals to come. We need to have the same attitude in our spiritual lives.

I am afraid far too many of us are trying to spiritually "drive ourselves to the hospital," instead of trusting the Lord. Preachers need a certain degree of confidence to lead people and step in front of them to teach God's Word. Yet there is a danger of trusting too much in our own abilities or the level of our faith. We think that it would never happen to us. We think our faith is too strong. We would never fall away. Yet Peter said the same thing the night he denied Jesus three times. "Therefore let anyone who thinks that he stands take heed lest he fall" (1 Cor. 10:12). We spend a great deal of time praying for others and their needs, but may not spend enough time praying about our own spiritual needs.

Jesus understood the value of prayer. The book of Luke is often described as the gospel of prayer. It talks more about the prayer life of Jesus than any other gospel. Luke 5:16 says of Jesus, "But Jesus Himself would often slip away to the wilderness and pray" (NASU).

Jesus prayed at the significant moments of his life. He prayed all night before choosing his disciples (Luke 6:12–13). Wouldn't you love to have been able to listen in on that conversation? I would like to have heard, in particular, the discussion concerning Peter and Judas. The apostles had the distinct privilege of listening to the Savior pray on numerous occasions. In fact, watching Jesus pray caused the apostles to ask Jesus to teach them how to pray (Luke 11:1ff). In light of this pattern of prayer in his own life, it should not surprise us that Jesus wanted his disciples to be people of prayer (Matt. 26:41). If the Son of God, the co-Creator of all that exists, felt the need to pray regularly, shouldn't we do the same?

Notice Eph. 6:18 once again, "Praying at all times in the Spirit, with all prayer and supplication. To that end keep alert with all perseverance, making supplication for all the saints." Remember that this statement follows Paul's discussion of the armor of God. The key to the armor is the power of God. It is his armor, not mine. We cannot conquer sin by our own power. We need God's help. I need to consider my prayer life. How often do I pray about the specific things that tempt me?

I also need to regularly confess my sins to the Father and seek his forgiveness (Jas. 5:16; 1 John 1:9). Our prayers can become routine and generic. We pray on autopilot; we rarely open up and "get real" with God. There is something healing and transformative that happens when we confess specific sins to God and ask for his help and forgiveness. The point is that we need God's help in our fight against sin.

We know the exact date it was painted: July 4, 1888. "Sunset at Montmajour" is a long-lost Van Gogh painting that collected dust in a Norwegian attic for many years. The 2013 discovery was the first full-sized canvas by the Dutch master to be discovered since 1928. Why did it languish in the dark for so long? Because they thought it was a fake. Research has now revealed that it is indeed genuine.

Paul told Timothy, "Let no one despise you for your youth, but set the believers an example in speech, in conduct, in love, in faith, in purity… Keep a close watch on yourself and on the teaching. Persist in this, for by so doing you will save both yourself and your hearers" (1 Tim. 4:12, 16). As leaders for the Lord, our sins not only inhibit our relationship with God; they can discourage the faith of others and lead them into the paths of unrighteousness. Satan knows that he has a better chance of defeating God's army if he can lead the Lord's leaders into sin. Those who listen to us are watching our lives to see if our faith is genuine. What they discover will determine whether our messages are put away in their "spiritual attics" or are put on display in their lives. Let us strive to make sure the faith they see is authentic.

9

the preacher
& his attitude

michael whitworth

I want you to imagine two very different preachers. The first is extremely polished in his delivery and quite gifted in his application. He's the kind of speaker that seems to make time stand still during his oratory—you never glance at your watch, and you forget all about your lunch plans or the big game kicking off at noon. His messages are the perfect blend of humor and conviction. Experienced homiletics teachers could learn from him. In every conceivable area of ministry, this man seems to excel. But there is one nagging factor that prevents him from becoming God's man.

His attitude.

The second preacher isn't as gifted in his speaking. In fact, he knows he's not as good as other preachers, but he gives it his best shot. He's not the most organized person in the world; a peek at his office warrants calling FEMA to the rescue! Nor is this preacher always accessible; he forgetfully leaves his cell phone behind some days, much to the chagrin of his elders and co-workers. All the same, his brethren overlook his oddities and personal failures because of one reason:

He has such a wonderful attitude.

I am convinced that no quality is more crucial to a preacher's success than his attitude. Learning to manage his time, his critics, his money, and his family are each important challenges in their own right. But a preacher's attitude can make him or break him. In this chapter, I intend to illustrate just how crucial our attitude is to our ministry, and particularly the attitude traits we should cultivate.

With the obvious exception being Christ, no minister I know has had a better attitude than that of the apostle Paul. His letters bear witness to his attitude in so many circumstances. In his counsel to Timothy and Titus, he spoke often about the need for the right attitude in the minister. His requirements for overseers mandated that such a man be gentle, rather than quarrelsome (1 Tim. 3:3; cf. 2 Tim. 2:24–25). Paul warned against teachers that craved controversy and quarrels, those that loved envy, dissension, slander, and evil suspicions (1 Tim. 6:4). He encouraged Timothy to adopt the attitude of a good soldier, an honest athlete, and a hard-working farmer. "Think over what I say, for the Lord will give you understanding in everything" (2 Tim. 2:3–7). Likewise, Paul charged Titus to teach sound doctrine. While that has become a byword for "right beliefs" among several religious groups, the immediate context has Paul mentioning things like sobriety, dignity, self-control, faithfulness, love, and steadfastness (Tit. 2:1–2).

In short, a preacher's attitude is just as important as his doctrine.

Our attitude matters because it reflects our heart. Jesus was clear, "What comes out of the mouth proceeds from the heart, and this defiles a person. For out of the heart come evil thoughts, murder, adultery, sexual immorality, theft, false witness, slander"

(Matt. 15:18–19). A poor attitude, like a poor mouth, reflects a poisoned heart. A preacher's polished exterior will eventually reveal the grime of a bad heart. The veneer will crack and the façade will decay. Instead of developing a sophisticated filter for our attitude, we should learn to cultivate a healthy heart instead. Solomon counseled, "Above all else, guard your heart, for everything you do flows from it" (Prov. 4:23 NIV).

Our attitude matters because it affects our effectiveness. It is amazing to me how receptive a person will be to a minister with a good attitude. He may not have any rhetorical or debating skills whatsoever, yet a man with a good attitude can effectively win others to Christ. He may not know as many Scriptures as the next preacher, and he may have all the eloquence of a child playing with pots and pans in the kitchen floor, but a good attitude can convict hearts. In 1 Cor. 12–14, Paul spent a lot of time discussing the various gifts of the Spirit. The Corinthians foolishly believed that spiritual maturity was proven by the practice of miraculous gifts; as a result, some had become arrogant. That's why Paul showed them a more excellent way (1 Cor. 12:31b). Love was to be desired as the greatest spiritual gift because agape love is the mark of true maturity.

Our attitude matters because it affects our ability to withstand trials. "A joyful heart is good medicine, but a crushed spirit dries up the bones" (Prov. 17:22). A pessimistic attitude will cripple a preacher almost as soon as he begins ministry. The honeymoon at a new congregation doesn't last forever, so when the storms of ministry begin, a minister's attitude can help buoy him. A negative outlook, on the other hand, makes Satan's job much easier. Lots of congregations have suffered years of setbacks because their minister had a bad attitude about adversity that prevented him from serving them effectively. He was so preoccupied with his own problems that he could not help the weak among his own brethren.

Our attitude matters because a negative attitude does not glorify the Lord. If I am the only one who ever knows about or is affected by my bad attitude, it is still wrong. As those created in God's image, preachers are called upon to reflect the glory of God and bring him praises with our lives. A bad attitude in the heart of a minister is symptomatic of someone too focused on himself and not enough on things above. Paul was a minister who sought to see Christ magnified in every way, life or death (Phil. 1:20); he sought to do all things to God's glory (1 Cor. 10:31).

What attitude traits should we cultivate? I think the fruit of the Spirit listed by Paul in Gal. 5 is a good starting point.

love

In 1 Cor. 13, Paul demonstrated just how important love is in the attitude and actions of a Christian. All the marks of mature Christianity, if emptied of love, are worthless, he says. You can be the most gifted communicator the world has known, or the most generous giver, or the most intelligent thinker, the most trusting saint, or the most willing of martyrs—without love, it gets you nowhere (1 Cor. 13:1–3).

As a child, my mom made me memorize this passage. For a long time, I wrestled with how these words could be true. I knew they had to be true because they were in the Bible. But my experience led me to think otherwise. We applaud great speakers, we memorialize generous givers, and we praise intelligent thinkers. We speak of trusting saints in hallowed tones and hero-worship the martyrs. Rarely, however, do we make a big fuss over excellent lovers.

Maybe we should, because true love is tough to cultivate. It's hard to develop patience and kindness in our love, to give others the benefit of the doubt and not delight in their shortcomings. It's hard not to be stuck on ourselves or not be too easily offended. Being a loving person is hard work.

But there may not be a command given more often than the one to love one another. It is certainly to be *the* identifying mark of Jesus' disciples (John 13:35). We can seek to restore New Testament Christianity in our worship, our leadership structures, or in any other category. But if we don't love, we have no legitimate claim to the "of Christ" designation on our church signs. "Anyone who does not love does not know God, because God is love" (1 John 4:8).

The most practical way to foster love in our attitude is to reflect regularly on love's definition in 1 Cor. 13 and to demonstrate public affection for our spiritual family. Since a preacher often cannot live near biological family members, loving the brethren "like family" can pay enormous dividends in countless ways. Even for introverts like myself, giving an enthusiastic handshake or warm hug to someone may communicate to them more love than they've received in a month of Sundays. It certainly goes a long way in proving to the world (and our own members) that the church of Christ knows no racial, linguistic, ethnic, political, socio-economic, or gender barriers.

joy

In 1 Thess. 5:16, Paul commanded his readers to "rejoice always." Elsewhere, he said our constant rejoicing is to be "in the Lord" (Phil. 4:4). I don't think this means that it's always wrong to be unhappy; there is a significant difference between happiness and joy. If you were to lose a family member suddenly, your fellow Christians would be disturbed to find you happy at the funeral home. No, happiness has to do with the circumstances of life. Joy, on the other hand, is that condition that emanates from being in a right relationship with God.

Our brethren need to see authentic joy modeled for them in our lives. My dad used to quip that we cannot expect people to partake of the Bread of Life when it appears it has given us indigestion. Godly joy is manifest in a positive attitude in any and all circumstances. Joy is a close cousin of peace in that it springs from the quiet confidence of knowing God is in control, that he will work all things to his glory and our good. Joy is the contentment found in knowing we are part of something greater than ourselves. Self-centered people can't know joy.

Beginning the practice of joy may be as simple as rehearsing the many reasons we have to be thankful in Christ. In him alone, after all, are all spiritual blessings (Eph. 1:3). Joy and gratitude are closely related; rejoicing and giving thanks are commands, part of God's will for us (1 Thess 5:16, 18).

Since focus on what we *don't* have is the greatest enemy of joy, focus now on what God *has* given you. Are you unhappy in your present congregation? God may still have work for you to do there. Are you unhappy with your present leaders? The Bible is replete with examples of how terrible it is when God's people are leaderless. Leadership is God's gift; he will provide. "Count your many blessings, name them one by one, and it will surprise you what the Lord hath done."

peace

In Phil. 4:7, Paul referred to a peace that "surpasses all understanding." This peace comes from God, and it is beyond our ability to fully comprehend. To effectively lead God's people through various storms, we must model such peace for them. This does not mean we resist conflict at every turn; sometimes, conflict must be dealt with aggressively. And true peace isn't found in the absence of conflict anyway. Rather, peace is the contentment found in knowing we are right where God wants us to be, doing exactly what God wants us to do.

Being a man of peace does not require you to be stoic or unflappable. You are, after all, human! But being both peaceful and a peacemaker requires you to adopt a long-range perspective on things. Some things just don't matter in light of eternity, so take all things to God in prayer, knowing he will help you determine which things need attention and which need simply to be forgotten. Regardless of how cordial we are, we will experience opposition at every turn, for Satan loves to oppose God's servants. Let us take our cue from Paul. "For this light momentary affliction is preparing for us an eternal weight of glory beyond all comparison, as we look not to the things that are seen but to the things that are unseen. For the things that are seen are transient, but the things that are unseen are eternal" (2 Cor. 4:17–18).

patience

"Lord, give me patience, and give it to me now," is a prayer I often heard my dad pray with tongue-in-cheek. Patience is not a virtue in American society. An instant-gratification society that started with Reader's Digest condensed books and microwaved meals has now evolved into an insatiable beast of blazing Internet speeds and ministry-in-a-box approaches to church work.

But a patient attitude in ministry can help guard us against frustration and disappointment. Noah preached for a long time to his wicked generation, yet he only led his wife, sons, and daughters-in-law into the ark of safety. I wonder how an aged Daniel felt when he saw all the progress he had made with

Nebuchadnezzar evaporate in the brash rebellion of Belshazzar. We often assume that preaching on a subject once or twice will cure what ails a congregation; when that doesn't happen, we begin to doubt either our effectiveness or our audience's faithfulness. But preaching is like planting crops and raising children (cf. Matt. 13:3–9; Gal. 4:19), two endeavors that require tremendous patience.

In my own life, I believe I have cultivated greater patience than my dad did, but this has not been easy. Whenever I catch myself being in a hurry (and often for no good reason whatsoever), I look for ways to intentionally impede my "progress." Standing in the longest line at Wal-Mart is often the cure I need, or intentionally running an errand at rush hour. Ask a football coach, "How can I become a better tackler or blocker?" and he'll tell you to tackle and block more. Want to become a more patient person? You can look for quick fixes all you want, but until you are willing to allow God to place you in moments that *demand* patience, you will never develop it.

kindness & goodness

Kindness may be better translated as "generous." There are a lot of demands on the preacher, but we cannot afford to be known as one who is not kind to everyone. Many preachers seem to fit in one of two categories. The first group always seems preoccupied with something else when you are engaged with them. They make you feel unimportant. The second, however, make you feel as if you matter more than anything else in the world. They are generous with their time, attention, and support. I want to be in this second group. But I confess I too easily decide I don't have time for something or someone, when the reality is that I just don't feel like being generous. A kind attitude will motivate us to seek out opportunities to "do good to everyone, and especially to those who are of the household of faith" (Gal. 6:10).

Goodness is a moral quality that our attitude must possess. If forced to draw a distinction, I'd say that kindness is an attitude we demonstrate to others; goodness is an attitude of our own hearts. Kindness is external; goodness is internal. That means goodness has to do with a sincere heart. Terrible as it is, not every preacher ministers to God's people for the right reasons. Some do it for the money (crazy, I know!), and others, for the prestige. What about you? When did you last have an honest heart-to-heart talk with yourself about your motive to preach?

Developing kindness and goodness in our attitude requires a constant prayer that God would soften us. There are situations that require preachers to have thick skin, to not take things personally. But taken to the extreme, a preacher can become so calloused that he loses his capacity to empathize. May God soften the preacher's heart towards the bereaved at the funeral home, the surgery patient in the hospital, and the benevolence case at the door. "Then they also will answer, saying, 'Lord, when did we see you hungry or thirsty or a stranger or naked or sick or in prison, and did not minister to you?' Then he will answer them, saying, 'Truly, I say to you, as you did not do it to one of the least of these, you did not do it to me'" (Matt. 25:44–45).

faithfulness

The most difficult achievement in the life of a Christian is to trust God in all things. Every one of the Old Testament heroes of faith had their moments of embarrassing weakness. Abraham lied to Pharaoh, Moses struck the rock, and David committed adultery with Bathsheba. Elijah ran to the desert, Jeremiah ranted at the heavens, and Jonah pouted under a withered vine. Thanks be to God that, "if we are faithless, he remains faithful—for he cannot deny himself" (2 Tim. 2:13)! Most certainly, there will be times when you struggle to trust your Lord.

But one of the greatest things you can do for your congregation is to model for them how to trust God, especially in difficult times. We can preach a thousand sermons on what it means to be faithful, but they need to see us living these principles out. "Show me," instead of "tell me."

Being faithful in trying times is made easier by two things: submission to God's sovereignty and acceptance that suffering is our lot in life. The Lord is in control of all things, and if we trust him, he promises to work all things to our good and his own glory (Rom. 8:28). The apostle Paul's ministry was characterized by faithful submission to God's will: "For none of us lives to himself, and none of us dies to himself. For if we live, we live to the Lord, and if we die, we die to the Lord. So then, whether we live or whether we die, we are the Lord's" (Rom. 14:7–8).

We must also accept the fact that, as Christians, we are called to suffer. "All who desire to live a godly life in Christ Jesus will be persecuted" (2 Tim. 3:12; cf. 1 Pet. 2:20–21). Suffering is in the job description of being a Christian, and even more so in the preacher's job description! Knowing that you have been called to this will help you have a faithful attitude in trials. If the Lord saw fit to warn us that we would suffer unjustly, doesn't it stand to reason that he can be trusted to lead us through the storms?

gentleness

Of all aspects of the Spirit's fruit, this is the one I'm least crazy about. I don't like thinking about being gentle. If any of you speak at my funeral, don't you dare get up and say, "Michael was gentle." I'm OK with "meek" or "mellow." Or "easy-going." Yeah, I like that, "easy-going." But not "gentle." Something about that word makes a man cringe.

All the same, it is an attitude trait we'd do well to cultivate. In 1 Thess. 2, Paul spoke of how he and Silas had been like infants with the Christians at Thessalonica, meaning they had been gentle. He also invoked the image of a mother nurturing her children (1 Thess. 2:7). I watch my wife with our newborn son, and I'm struck with how gentle she is with him. She is much more patient than I when he is fussy or tired. She is sensitive to his moods and seems to know exactly what he needs in a given situation. She is gentle.

In our ministries, we will encounter all types of problem people. Some who are simply stubborn and rebellious need a spiritual 2x4 upside their head; sometimes "tough love" is in order (e.g. 1 Cor. 5). But a seasoned minister knows when gentleness, more so than toughness, is required (cf. 1 Thess. 5:14). Developing a gentle spirit will help you in times of conflict. There is a reason Solomon said, "A gentle answer turns away wrath, but a harsh word stirs up anger" (Prov. 15:1 NIV).

Some bullies go out looking to pick a fight; a gentle spirit can, at the very least, expose them for what they are and keep a contentious moment from becoming a congregational free-for-all. For those who are spiritually weak or just high-strung, a gentle spirit can encourage them. I know several men who exhibit special tenderness with their opponents, even when they are attacked personally. I am thankful for their example.

Maybe being known at my funeral as possessing a gentle attitude wouldn't be such a bad thing, after all!

self-control

This has arguably been the greatest flaw in my attitude. Most of us don't even think about our self-control, especially in relation to our attitude. But the longer I live, the more I realize the mind is a powerful thing, something that must be harnessed for good, or Satan will exploit it for evil. In 2 Cor. 10:5, Paul wrote, "We destroy arguments and every lofty opinion raised against the knowledge of God, and take every thought captive to obey Christ." The greatest area in which the minister may need to exercise self-control is in his thoughts and attitude.

On Sunday night or Monday morning—the times when you feel lowest—your heart becomes fertile ground for Satan's malicious lies. No one loves or appreciates you. The elders don't know what they're doing; they probably couldn't even tie their own shoelaces. You'll never do anything important; you'll never make a difference in this congregation or community. Take these thoughts captive, soldier, and bring them to your Commander-in-Chief! Exercising self-control in our attitude means looking at things through Jesus' eyes. As long as he is Lord, things are never as bad as we think.

Finally, I want to pass on some advice for developing and maintaining a healthy attitude as God's messenger and minister.

Watch your influences. Some of us need to follow the same advice we might give our kids. Some of your family or friends may be poisoning your attitude against members, elders, the church, or ministry in general, etc. I've started to note those people who seemingly leave me more downcast and pessimistic after I've spent time with them. We also know men and women who, in the span of only a few minutes, can inspire and motivate us by a positive attitude. Spend time with these good people, soak up their enthusiasm, and bask in their positive attitude.

Read the Bible. This advice may seem akin to "Take two aspirin and call me in the morning," but spending quality time with the Word of God will help shift our attitude. I can speak from personal experience that, when I've gone a long time without really reading my Bible, my attitude is the first to suffer. I become joyless, my temper shortens, and my patience wears thin. Yet reading God's Word constantly offers an attitude adjustment of which I'm in desperate need. It is always a humbling experience, but also a fortifying one—like a tune-up for your car or a check-up at the doctor.

Pray. Specifically, pray that God will spotlight those attitudes that need to change. I'm reminded of the story of a large factory that once had a broken piece of machinery and called an expert in to look it over and fix it. He came in, looked the machine over for about ten minutes, fiddled with it a little, and soon had it running good as new. In the invoice he later sent, he charged $15,000, a much larger sum in those days. The factory owner balked and demanded an itemized invoice to know how the expert justified so exorbitant an expense. The reply came back: "Fixing the problem: $1. Knowing what needed to be fixed: $14,999." It's possible we may not know what in our attitude needs fixing, but the Lord does. Diligent prayer will expose where we need to grow in this regard.

Remember, O man of God, that a lot is riding on your attitude. Most of all, maintaining a healthy attitude will bring glory to your Father in heaven, and you will never know greater joy than this.

10

the preacher & laziness
steve higginbotham

It was 10:00 am when my cell phone rang. I picked the phone up on the fourth ring so that I could finish typing my sentence, lest I lose my train of thought. On the other end of the line was a Christian lady whose first words were, "Steve, I hope I didn't call too early and get you out of bed, but I was wondering if you could…"

Call too early?

Get me out of bed?

It was 10:00 in the morning! What job allows a person to stay in bed that late? Did this sister in Christ really think I might still be in bed at that hour? I wanted to take a moment right then and there and tell her all the things I had already accomplished that day, but I bit my tongue.

I received another call from a lady about 1:30 pm. She said, "Steve, I have a hair appointment at the beauty shop at 2:00 pm. Could you take me? Everyone else I know has jobs and is working." Once again, I found myself dazed by the perception. Did this Christian lady not understand that I too had a job?

And then there's the playful, jovial banter preachers sometimes hear—comments like, "Wow, what a job! You only have to work one day a week!" Or, "It must be nice to only have to work three hours on Sunday and one hour on Wednesday night and get paid that large salary!"

Let me share a word of caution and advice to preachers about this "playful" banter. I believe that such talk is harmful in a number of ways, and we shouldn't be party to it. First and foremost, this sort of banter disrespects God's plan (1 Cor. 1:21; 9:7–11). It is God's divine arrangement that allows preachers to be supported so that they can preach full-time and not be distracted by secular employment.

This banter also chips away at the preacher's respect and authority. One who proclaims the saving message of the gospel has a far too important responsibility to allow himself to be on the receiving end of jokes that make him and his work the object of ridicule. And if this weren't enough, this sort of joking has a long-lasting impact on others. How many young men will want to grow up to be a preacher one day if all they have heard and seen is contempt and ridicule directed at preachers? Not many young boys will grow up to become what their parents hold in contempt, even if they are "just joking."

Therefore, I try to politely dismiss these types of remarks. But how do I do that without alienating people? Here's what I say: "You know, you're right. I do have one of the easiest jobs anyone could possibly have, because my job is to go around bragging on Jesus, and how hard can that be?" There's not much anyone can say in response to this, and it generally brings an end to the disrespectful banter.

Although I have not heard these kinds of statements through the years, I know they are not uncommon, and I find that somewhat troublesome. It causes me to wonder if people are really that uninformed regarding the day-to-day work of a preacher, or if they have been given some reason to think preachers are lazy. I'm afraid that the latter may be the case, that laziness has been a stumbling block to many preachers and has given preaching a bad name. Due to the nature of the work of preaching, preachers must be independent, a self-starter, and must practice self-discipline. Frequently, preachers have an arrangement with a congregation that requires very little accountability for what they do on a day-to-day basis, and consequently, more than a few preachers have developed lazy habits that are harmful to him, his reputation, the church, and a lost world.

In this chapter, it is my aim to appeal to preachers to avoid laziness, to do some honest self-evaluation, and to share a few tips that will help us overcome the stumbling block of laziness.

reasons to avoid laziness

There's too much work to be done. There are seven billion people living on this planet, most of whom do not have a relationship with Jesus. There's more work to do, and this work is urgent! While we may attempt to dismiss the obligation of reaching seven billion people by simply saying it's beyond our ability, every day, closer to home, we can pick up our evening newspaper and read the obituaries of people who have died outside of Christ.

On August 6, 1945, a doctor was walking to work in Hiroshima when the city was bombed. This doctor was far enough away to survive the bombing, but as he walked toward the city, he saw the staggering, devastating injuries. Thousands of men, women, and children were terribly burned and wounded. He felt overwhelmed. How could he possibly help so many people when he was just one doctor, and all he had was his small doctor's bag? He couldn't, but he could do *something*. So the doctor knelt down to help one of the wounded at his feet. Like this doctor, we mustn't allow the size of "seven billion" to overwhelm us into doing nothing. While we cannot minister to seven billion, there is still much work to be done at our feet.

Laziness will cause you to miss opportunities. I have often contemplated what might have happened if Philip hadn't run to the Ethiopian nobleman (Acts 8:30)? According to the text, Philip had to "overtake" his chariot. If Philip had been lazy and drug his feet, kicking up sand as he moped along the way, he would have missed this opportunity to teach this man about Jesus.

Several years ago, I heard a preacher tell of an incident that had happened to him. The preacher had been conducting a Bible study with a neighbor. One evening, he received a call from that neighbor. It was past suppertime, and the preacher didn't want to be bothered, so he allowed the call to go to voicemail. The next morning, the preacher received a call from the same number, but it was from the wife of the man with whom he had been studying. She was hysterical. Her husband had died that morning of a massive heart attack, and she was calling to ask him to perform his funeral. After he hung up the phone, he remembered he had a voicemail from the night before that he had not yet listened to. What he heard made him physically sick. This man left a message that said, "I've been giving a lot of thought to our studies, and I want to be baptized into Christ and become a Christian. Let me know when you can baptize me." This preacher was shaken and wept uncontrollably when he heard the message. That day, he asked God's forgiveness and vowed to be more aware of the opportunities he has to bring people to Jesus.

Laziness isn't victimless. It will mean the difference between heaven and hell for someone.

You owe it to those supporting you. Remember that you and your family are being supported by the generosity of the Christians to whom you are ministering. I'm not suggesting that you are a charity case, and that the salary you receive isn't earned. Quite the contrary. What a preacher is paid is wages earned, not benevolence (1 Cor. 9:6–11; Gal. 6:6). But the wages a preacher earns comes from the labor and sacrifice of his fellow Christians. How can we betray that sacrifice through laziness? Laziness shows contempt and ingratitude toward those who are making financial sacrifices for you.

Laziness will cause you to become a hindrance. No one has respect for a lazy person. If a preacher develops a reputation for being lazy, his character and influence for good will be destroyed. If that happens, what does a preacher have left to contribute to a congregation? A preacher needs to be a man of character and respect because the message he proclaims demands nothing less. A preacher cannot allow himself to get in the way of the message he is presenting, but laziness will do just that. If a preacher is lazy, he won't be heard. His message will fall on deaf ears. In fact, when one proclaims one thing and lives another, not only will people not listen, but they will develop contempt for the message being preached, as well as the God behind the message (Rom. 2:24).

This work demands your best. Don't ever forget what your job is—you are a representative for God! What an honor to give your life to being God's spokesman! We live in a culture where God's voice is being increasingly silenced. Where are the preachers? Where is God's voice? Who will stand up and be counted? God needs courageous men to counter culture with truth, to slay error with the sword of the Spirit, and to fight the good fight of faith. Laziness will prevent us from doing this.

Several years ago, our local newspaper, one with a

circulation of nearly 30,000, dedicated a full page once a week to religion. What an opportunity to reach so many in our community without spending a dime! But week after week went by, and the dozen or more preachers in our area were not using this page. I finally encouraged one preacher-friend to take advantage of this opportunity to be a moral voice in our community. He declined my encouragement and said, "It takes too much work to write." Yes, it takes work, but that's the work we've chosen for ourselves—to be God's spokesmen! Let us be sure to give God our very best effort.

We must answer to God. Will a man rob God (Mal. 3:8)? We are stewards of heavenly treasures, and we will some day answer to God for our stewardship (1 Cor. 4:1–2). I frequently think of these passages as I go about my work.

Jesus held in contempt the religious leaders of his day who were little more than figureheads of religion and spirituality, but inwardly they were full of extortion and self-indulgence (Matt. 23:35). These corrupt religious leaders, supported by the tithes of religious people, were the recipients of the strongest recorded criticism Jesus ever offered. Because of that, I frequently examine myself and seek God's forgiveness for shortcomings with regard to the use of my time, talents, and stewardship. I don't ever want to forget that I will someday answer to God for my stewardship. I cannot afford to be lazy if I want to be found a faithful steward.

The Bible explicitly condemns laziness. Consider what the wise man said: "I passed by the field of a sluggard, by the vineyard of a man lacking sense, and behold, it was all overgrown with thorns; the ground was covered with nettles, and its stone wall was broken down. Then I saw and considered it; I looked and received instruction. A little sleep, a little slumber, a little folding of the hands to rest, and poverty will come upon you like a robber, and want like an armed man" (Prov. 24:30–34). Is it possible for us to have effective ministries when we behave as those who lack sense?

Self-examination is useful, frequently needed, and seldom practiced. It's especially important when it pertains to spiritual matters. Through the process of self-examination, we can identify our shortcomings if we're honest with ourselves. One of the worst things we can do is live a life that isn't monitored or reviewed. It's this process of review that teaches us not to repeat our mistakes. Could it be that we are lazy, or have tendencies that lead to laziness? If so, we need to expunge these characteristics from our lives. Below are a few ways in which laziness manifests itself. Do some self-examination.

manifestations of laziness

Failing to read and stay informed. A preacher needs to be a man constantly reading. How can we refresh the spirits of those who assemble to hear us when our own bucket is empty? Reading fills our buckets with truths, ideas, insights, and illustrations to help the Word of God resonate in people. A preacher who won't read won't stay fresh for very long. He will soon resort to lazy practices in his sermon preparation. Read the Bible regularly. Read good books. Pay attention to news and cultural trends. View life through a spiritual lens that finds spiritual truths and biblical principles in the ordinary and routine. Who have you read lately? What blogs or books have you read recently? What cultural trend have you recently addressed in a sermon or in writing? Failure to remain fresh and relevant is a sign of laziness.

Failure to adequately prepare lessons. Without adequate study, sermons and lessons are shallow. They fail to challenge or provide insight. They will lack passion in their presentation.

For a number of years, I have run a website on which I make

available many of my sermon outlines. It's amazing to me to watch my web stats on Saturday night. They jump off the chart! I interpret those statistics to mean that there are many preachers waiting until the very last minute to prepare their sermon for the next day. While I make those outlines available to help preachers, I don't intend for them to be grabbed on Saturday night and used as a crutch with which to get through Sunday.

When Sunday rolls around, do we enter the pulpit because we have to say something, or because we have something to say? The answer to that question will give you a clue as to whether you've been lazy through the week.

Sleeping late. Solomon said, "Love not sleep, lest you come to poverty" (Prov. 20:13). Not only will this rob you of valuable time; it is a symptom of laziness that you can't hide from others. Because preachers don't punch a time clock, they must possess self-discipline and be a self-starter. Good or bad, habits are hard to break. Why not make this truth work for you? Develop the habit of being an early riser. Get out of bed; there's work to do!

Playing on the computer. While the computer has become an essential tool in my preaching work, I have also found it can be one of the biggest stumbling blocks leading toward laziness. It's easy to neglect your work by spending hours surfing the Internet or commenting on your favorite social media site. I'm a user of Facebook and other social media outlets, but I sometimes wonder how many collective hours are wasted by preachers who seem to spend their entire day posting and waiting for others to respond to their posts. Don't justify "wasting time" by saying you're just trying to stay in touch with members. Certainly staying in touch is good, but there comes a time when you need to pour yourself into thought, prayer, and study. You can't do that when you feel the need to respond or view what was written every time your computer dings. Turn social media off!

Failure to visit. Failing to visit members in need is a sign of laziness. Visiting requires effort and is seldom convenient. Yes, I know that visiting can interrupt your study, and that your train of thought can be disrupted. And yes, I know that you'll sometimes be in the middle of something and have to leave it undone. But while these things are true, we need to remember that people take precedence. People shouldn't be viewed as a disruption or inconvenience to our schedule and purpose; people are our purpose! However, laziness will provide us with many excuses to keep us from visiting and fulfilling our purpose.

Failure to get involved with others. Laziness will sometimes cause us to shy away from events that we don't "have to" attend. While I know there is no way a preacher can be involved in everything a congregation is doing, I also know that laziness can keep him from being a part of some of the activities in which the congregation is involved.

A few years ago, a church building was burned to the ground by an arsonist. The brethren there were undaunted. They began meeting every weekend to rebuild the building themselves. Both the men and women showed up. Then men worked on the building, while the women provided picnic lunches for them. It was a period of great bonding, and in a matter of months, they had rebuilt their church building. However, during their rebuilding process, the preacher never once showed up to any of these workdays. He said he wasn't skilled at that sort of labor. Maybe he couldn't drive a nail or crosscut a board, but he could carry a board, refill nails, and a dozen other things that would have been helpful. His laziness embittered the congregation and cost him his job. Laziness can keep you from taking advantage of opportunities to be with your brethren.

Dreading an elders' meeting. If a preacher finds himself dreading a scheduled meeting with his elders, it may be an indication of guilt born out of laziness. Elders' meetings are nothing to be feared. In fact, they are an opportunity to be encouraged and to stack hands on the work that is before you. But when one knows he has been slacking off; when one knows he's not done what was expected of him; when one knows he's been lazy, he might develop a sense of dread or uneasiness. If you experience that sense of dread, maybe it's your conscience telling on you.

If, after reading the above signs of laziness and doing some honest self-examination, you feel a twinge of conviction, what should you do about it? The following are some specific actions that will help prevent laziness.

overcoming laziness

Partner with someone to do the undesirable. If you find a particular part of your work distasteful and difficult to do, then partner with someone who can help you fulfill that task. For example, maybe you find visiting the nursing home very depressing and discouraging. Consequently, you procrastinate and frequently leave the task undone if it is left up to you to do it. If that's the case, find a brother, co-worker, or an elder to go with you. Maybe you could even designate a particular day each month when visits will be made. The accountability will help you fulfill what you might otherwise fail to do. Solomon said, "Two are better than one, because they have a good reward for their toil. For if they fall, one will lift up his fellow. But woe to him who is alone when he falls and has not another to lift him up!" (Eccl. 4:9–10).

Fall more deeply in love with Jesus. We do not consider difficult the work we do for those we love. Why? Because it's a labor of love (Heb. 6:10). We've all seen husbands and wives minister day and night to their ailing spouses. We've seen mothers sit up all night with a child with a fever. Yet they do so without complaint because it's a labor of love. As we grow closer and closer to Jesus, we will love him more and more, and the work required of us will become easier and easier to accomplish.

In 1922, Helen Lemmel penned the following words: "Turn your eyes upon Jesus / Look full in his wonderful face / And the things of earth will grow strangely dim / In the light of his glory and grace." How true! When we turn our eyes upon Jesus, how can we not love him? And such love, as it grows and matures, makes the peripheral things on earth that have a tendency to distract us, grow dimmer and dimmer.

I have frequently heard major league baseball players speak incredulously about their salaries. They say, "I can't believe I'm getting paid to do what I love to do! How could it get any better?" It's this same sentiment that can be said of one who falls deeply in love with Jesus. When one is in love with Jesus, work isn't "work." It's a privilege. Laziness will not exist in one who deeply loves Jesus.

Remember what's at stake. If we could only see the end from the beginning with the same clarity with which the Lord can see (Isa. 46:10), we wouldn't give in to the temptations of life. If the husband could only see the hurt that his infidelity created in his life, as well as in the lives of those he loves, he wouldn't be unfaithful. If the drunkard lying in the gutter could only see where alcohol would take him and what it would cost him, he would have never taken the first drink. If a mother could only see what impact her unfaithfulness to the Lord would have on the eternal destiny of her children, she would never be unfaithful. And if a preacher could only see what laziness will cost him, his brethren, the lost world, and his God, he would never succumb to the temptation to be lazy.

Laziness in a preacher comes at a cost. The stakes are high. What hangs in the balance are such things as whether we will have a good or bad reputation, whether we will miss or take advantage of open doors of opportunity, whether we will be effective or ineffective in our ministry, whether we will be found as a faithful or unfaithful steward, and whether we will help or hinder others. In short, heaven and hell are at stake!

M ay God help us not to be near-sighted. Rather, may we be men of clear and full vision. May we be stirred by the lost. May we, like Paul, be provoked by our yearning to save the lost from their ignorance and sin (Acts 17:16).

May we understand that Jesus needs us! I almost choke up at the words, but it's true. Jesus needs me! Jesus doesn't need me intrinsically, but he has shown his need for me by placing in my hands his gospel of salvation. Paul said the church, of which I am a part as an individual, is "his body, the fullness of him who fills all in all" (Eph. 1:23). Jesus is incomplete, not in his person, but in his purpose if the church doesn't fulfill her responsibility of being God's point-of-contact with the world. Surely, such an awesome responsibility can only be received by doing our very best in his service.

Finally, may it be said of us what was said of the Lord, "Zeal for your house will consume me" (John 2:17).

11

the preacher & his core
chris mccurley

One of the biggest buzzwords in the realm of fitness is "core." A number of training regimens focus on strengthening one's core. Anatomically, the core refers to the abdominal muscles, mid and lower back, obliques, gluteus maximus, and upper legs. The core has become a point of emphasis because many fitness gurus believe this part of the human body is vital to everything one does. Therefore, the stronger the core, the stronger and healthier the individual.

When it comes to the preacher he, too, must have a strong core. The core is vital to everything he does. If his core is weak, the health of his ministry suffers. The preacher can be a time-management expert. He may be a loving husband and a godly father. He may be well liked by the members of the congregation. He may be a terrific communicator and eloquent orator. He may be a best-selling author and a sought-after lecturer.

But if he neglects his core, he is a miserable failure.

The preacher wears many hats. Oftentimes, he's a preacher, a teacher, a writer, a therapist, a counselor, an encourager, etc. Outside of his responsibilities to the church, he may be a husband, a father, a community leader, a secular employee, etc. Whatever hat the preacher wears, he must never forget that there is a difference between what he does and who he is. At his core, he is not all the things I just mentioned. At his core, he is a Christian. Everything he does relates to his core. That being said, the stronger his core, the stronger he will be in everything else.

core values

1. It's not about you. Unfortunately, I have known preachers who were more concerned about the letters following their name than the mission of Christ. Some preachers care more about the spotlight than being a light for Christ. Some preachers have allowed a love for the world to overshadow a love for the Lord. "Preacher" is a designation. "Christian" is our identity, and our identity drives what we do.

Jesus said in John 8:54, "If I glorify myself, my glory is nothing. It is my Father who glorifies me, of whom you say, 'He is our God.'" Jesus' number one priority was to glorify God in all he did. Is that our number one goal? At our core must be an intense desire to please God and glorify him in everything that we do. The moment this ceases to be our goal, we fail.

In John 5:30, Jesus said: "I can do nothing on my own. As I hear, I judge, and my judgment is just, because I seek not my own will but the will of him who sent me." Preaching is not about me! A life of ministry is not about what I can accomplish with God working alongside me. Rather, it's about what God can accomplish by working through me. I am not the focal point; I am the vessel. We are nothing on our own. Any success we may have must be attributed to God and what he can do when we make ourselves available to him. It is vital that we understand who we work for. It is not the members. It is not the elders. It is God. May his will always be done!

2. *It's about the message.* A cursory look through Scripture reveals many preachers who faced adversity. Jeremiah was one such preacher. This prophet was commissioned to deliver a message from God to a people who didn't want to hear it. The Jewish people had become fat and sassy. They were satisfied spiritually, and that is always a precarious predicament. Even worse, they had turned to the worship of idols, all the while continuing to worship in the temple. Jeremiah 7:8–11 gives a description of the heart of the people:

> Behold, you trust in deceptive words to no avail. Will you steal, murder, commit adultery, swear falsely, make offerings to Baal, and go after other gods that you have not known, and then come and stand before me in this house, which is called by my name, and say, "We are delivered!"—only to go on doing all these abominations? Has this house, which is called by my name, become a den of robbers in your eyes? Behold, I myself have seen it, declares the LORD.

Jeremiah's mission was to tell the people of God that Jehovah would no longer tolerate their incessant sin. An enemy was coming who would destroy their city and take them captive. The people responded to God's message, delivered through the prophet, by mocking him. There were insults and threats. We read later that the priest, Pashhur, had Jeremiah beaten and put in stocks (Jer. 20:2). Keep in mind that these weren't pagan extremists; these were religious folks.

> O LORD, you have deceived me, and I was
> deceived; you are stronger than I, and you have
> prevailed. I have become a laughingstock all the
> day; everyone mocks me. For whenever I speak,
> I cry out, I shout, "Violence and destruction!"
> For the word of the LORD has become for me a
> reproach and derision all day long.
>
> Jer. 20:7–8

Jeremiah was a preacher under fire. I doubt many men filling the pulpit in America have ever had to fear for their lives, yet Jeremiah did. He faced extreme disappointment and discouragement, torture and torment. The message and the mission were not of his choosing. This is not something he had asked for.

> Cursed be the day on which I was born! The day
> when my mother bore me, let it not be blessed!
> Cursed be the man who brought the news to my
> father, "A son is born to you," making him very
> glad. Let that man be like the cities that the LORD
> overthrew without pity; let him hear a cry in the
> morning and an alarm at noon, because he did
> not kill me in the womb; so my mother would
> have been my grave, and her womb forever great.
> Why did I come out from the womb to see toil
> and sorrow, and spend my days in shame?
>
> Jer. 20:14–18

"I wish I had never been born," Jeremiah exclaimed. "It would have been better to have died in my mother's womb, rather than carry out this calling." The prophet is at his personal ground zero. He has plumbed the depths of despair, crumbled under the weight of preaching this message to an obstinate people. Who could blame him for giving up? But in the midst of personal turmoil, Jeremiah utters these words: "If I say, 'I will not mention him, or speak any more in his name,' there is in my heart as it were a burning fire shut up in my bones, and I am weary with holding it in, and I cannot" (Jer. 20:9).

One might say Jeremiah was in a no-win situation. If he continued to preach the message, he would continue to endure persecution, perhaps even death. But the Word of God burned so intensely inside of him that he could not quit. The message had consumed him. He felt it in the marrow of his bones. In all his misery, he could not ignore the mission. Despite the immense mental, emotional, and physical pain that preaching the message garnered, he couldn't hold it in. He couldn't ignore it.

He had to speak.

What was this fire in Jeremiah's bones? Do we have the same fire? Jeremiah had an intense desire to glorify God. Why else would he continue on in the face of such personal distress? At his core was the desire to please God, and that desire trumped everything else, even personal comfort.

3. It's about Christ. In 2 Cor. 11, Paul defended his apostleship. He found it utterly ridiculous to have to list his credentials, but he felt the need to do so because false teachers were discrediting him while leading Christians astray. Paul presented a resume that magnifies a life and ministry beyond compare.

> Are they servants of Christ? I am a better one—I am talking like a madman—with far greater labors, far more imprisonments, with countless beatings, and often near death. Five times I received at the hands of the Jews the forty lashes less one. Three times I was beaten with rods. Once I was stoned. Three times I was shipwrecked; a night and a day I was adrift at sea; on frequent journeys, in danger

> from rivers, danger from robbers, danger from my
> own people, danger from Gentiles, danger in
> the city, danger in the wilderness, danger at sea,
> danger from false brothers; in toil and hardship,
> through many a sleepless night, in hunger and
> thirst, often without food, in cold and exposure.
> And, apart from other things, there is the daily
> pressure on me of my anxiety for all the churches.
> Who is weak, and I am not weak? Who is made
> to fall, and I am not indignant?
>
> 2 Cor. 11:23–29

Like Jeremiah, Paul was well acquainted with the rigors of ministry. He was intimately familiar with the trials and tribulations associated with spreading the gospel message. Yet he persevered. He pressed on. Why? Because at his core was Jesus Christ and an intense desire to share the gospel. Beatings, stonings, and shipwrecks could not affect his essence. "I have been crucified with Christ. It is no longer I who live, but Christ who lives in me. And the life I now live in the flesh I live by faith in the Son of God, who loved me and gave himself for me" (Gal. 2:20).

Paul's life and ministry had nothing to do with Paul. It was all about Jesus. Paul had been crucified with Christ. The old Paul was dead and buried; the new Paul had a new core—Christ. That is why he could endure the unthinkable and do the unbelievable. In Phil. 4:11–13 he writes:

> Not that I am speaking of being in need, for I have
> learned in whatever situation I am to be content.
> I know how to be brought low, and I know how
> to abound. In any and every circumstance, I have
> learned the secret of facing plenty and hunger,
> abundance and need. I can do all things through
> him who strengthens me.

What was the secret to Paul's contentment? Christ. Paul had all he really needed. God's preacher needs to realize this as well. We are adequately supplied. We can press on in the midst of trials knowing our core is strong.

There is great value in recognizing who you are not. The preacher is many things, but he is not superman. Be realistic when it comes to your role. Challenges are a guarantee. Trials are inevitable. Where you have people, you have problems, and the church certainly follows this principle. Discouragement is not hard to find. In fact, it will typically find you. Remember who you serve first. Remember the source of your strength. Remember that you are human. Far too many preachers suppress their feelings of weakness. They feel as though they must put on a façade or wear a mask so that the congregation knows that they are strong. They're trying to live up to a standard that's unrealistic—one that suggests they have it all together and are exempt from struggles. Remember Paul's words:

> For I do not understand my own actions. For I do not do what I want, but I do the very thing I hate. Now if I do what I do not want, I agree with the law, that it is good. So now it is no longer I who do it, but sin that dwells within me. For I know that nothing good dwells in me, that is, in my flesh. For I have the desire to do what is right, but not the ability to carry it out. For I do not do the good I want, but the evil I do not want is what I keep on doing. Now if I do what I do not want, it is no longer I who do it, but sin that dwells within me.
>
> Rom. 7:15–20

What did the original audience think when they heard this for the first time? Why would Paul share such a personal account of his struggles? Is this not ill-advised? He was a fearless leader, someone that fledgling and mature Christians alike looked up to. Wouldn't such words ruin his credibility?

One Sunday, when I was attending church in Arkansas, the preacher delivered a soul-stirring message—one of those sermons that didn't just step on your toes; it stepped on your heart. Upon offering the invitation, one of the elders came forward. With tears in his eyes and a lump in his throat, he admitted to dealing with sin in his life. He confided in his church family about how difficult it was to be a shepherd and to live up to that standard. He asked the church to pray for him as he sought to be a better leader and, more importantly, a better Christian. Because of the respect this man had among the congregation, and because of his character and reputation, many people were surprised to see him come forward. If any person had it all together, it had to be him. In answering the invitation and baring his heart, he made a tremendous impact on our church family. It brought us closer together. It galvanized us. This elder exemplified for us what it means to be vulnerable and to let others in.

Sometimes transparency is needed. Obviously, we shouldn't share everything. Some things are meant to be private. Transparency is not an excuse to be a dump truck and unload everything on others, but the preacher should be able to be vulnerable. He should be able to share his hurts and struggles when appropriate. Otherwise, his core will never be strengthened.

What are some practical ways the preacher can strengthen his core? The following are a few helpful hints.

- ***Be devoted to prayer and personal Bible study.***
  Don't let sermon preparation time be the only

time you study God's word.

- **Be still.** As stated in the opening chapter, find time to hit the "pause" button. It may seem counterintuitive to get away from the church, but preachers need time to be with their family, to relax, to enjoy leisure time, or to just be still.

- **Be weak and vulnerable.** Share your struggles with your elders or a close friend in the church. You're not superman. Don't pretend you are. Take off the mask and be real.

- **Be resilient.** The next time you receive unwarranted criticism; the next time you feel under-appreciated; the next time you have your feelings hurt by a church member, remember who you serve above all others—God. Think of Jeremiah and Paul. Don't run from the pulpit when you experience hardship. Stay focused on your Maker and the mission.

- **Be Christ.** I often hear Christians claim that the goal in this life is to get to heaven. But I believe the goal is to be like Christ. If you pursue that goal with your entire being, the destination will never be in question. Like Christ, preach the truth. Show compassion. Despise sin, but love the sinner. Be about the Father's business. Glorify God in all you do!

Paul's dying words to the young preacher Timothy were, "Preach the word; be ready in season and out of season; reprove, rebuke, and exhort, with complete patience and teaching" (2 Tim. 4:2). The apostle went on to write:

> For I am already being poured out as a drink offering, and the time of my departure has come. I have fought the good fight, I have finished the race, I have kept the faith. Henceforth there is laid up for me the crown of righteousness, which the Lord, the righteous judge, will award to me on that Day, and not only to me but also to all who have loved his appearing.
>
> 2 Tim. 4:6–8

Preach the word brothers! Fight the good fight of faith! Finish the course, and I'll see you in heaven!

May God bless the preacher!

about the authors

Chris McCurley has been in ministry for 13 years. He currently serves as preaching minister for the Oldham Lane church of Christ in Abilene, TX. He is the husband of Libby and the father to Keely, Zoe, and Zane. He is an avid fan of the Dallas Cowboys, the St. Louis Cardinals, and relaxing in the mountains.

Neal Pollard has been preaching for more than 25 years and currently serves as the pulpit minister for the Bear Valley church of Christ in Denver, CO. He and his wife, Kathy, have three sons. Neal enjoys watching sports, running, weightlifting, hiking, and traveling.

Jacob Hawk serves as the pulpit minister for Riverside Church of Christ in Kerrville, TX. He also hosts Riverside's television program, *The Bread of Life*. He and his wife, Natalie, have one son, as well as a beautiful baby on the way. Jacob is also the author of *Image of the Invisible God*. In addition to preaching, writing, and ministry, he loves to spend time with his family and play golf.

Jay Lockhart has been preaching for over 50 years. He currently serves as an elder and the preaching minister for the

Whitehouse, TX Church of Christ. Jay and his wife, Arlene, have three adult children and six grandchildren. He has a passion for preaching and appears on numerous lectureships, seminars, and gospel meetings each year.

Jeff A. Jenkins has been preaching for 40 years and currently serves as the preaching minister for the Lewisville, TX Church of Christ. He and his wife, Laura, have two children and two grandchildren. He is the author of *God's Plan for Unity* and co-editor of *Redeeming the Times* and *Reaching for Passion*. His favorite hobbies are reading and spending time with his family.

Adam Faughn is the pulpit minister for the Lebanon Road Church of Christ in Nashville, TN. He and his wife, Leah, are blessed with two children, Mary Carol and Turner. In addition to preaching, Adam maintains a blog (faughnfamily.com) and writes materials for 24:15 Publications (faughnfamily.com/store). He enjoys reading, college basketball, and one-hit wonders.

Dale Jenkins is the pulpit minister for the Spring Meadows church in Spring Hill, TN. He has preached for nearly 35 years and has two sons who are ministers. He and his wife, Melanie, also have two grandchildren. Dale loves encouraging preachers in every way he can and enjoys being a part of The Jenkins Institute where many of his shorter writings can be found. Most of his longer writings have not been written yet.

Kirk Brothers spent 23 years in local ministry before becoming a professor of Bible at Freed-Hardeman University in 2010. He serves as a part-time missionary to Latin America, training preachers and starting Future Minister Training Camps for teenage boys. He also works with the college and young professionals group at the 4th Street church of Christ in Selmer, TN. Kirk and his wife, Cindy, have two daughters.

Michael Whitworth preaches for the church in Bowie, TX. He is the founder of Start2Finish Books and the author of several works, including *The Derision of Heaven* and the award-winning *The Epic of God*. He also blogs regularly at start2finishblog. com. He loves M&Ms and large Mason jars. In his spare time, Michael enjoys drinking coffee, watching sports, and spending time with his awesome family and furry golden retriever.

Steve Higginbotham has been preaching full-time since his graduation from Freed-Hardeman in 1984. He presently serves as the pulpit minister for the Karns Church of Christ in Knoxville, TN. He also serves as an instructor at the Southeast Institute of Biblical Studies. Steve and his wife, Kim, have four children. He is a fan of the Pittsburgh Steelers, likes to golf, and is quite proficient in Mayberry trivia.

acknowledgments
from the editor

To my wife, Libby.
You are an exemplary mother and spouse.
Thank you for your love, strength and support.
But thank you most of all for leading me to Christ.
Without you, I truly would be lost.

To my children, Keely, Zoe, and Zane.
I love you with all my heart.
You are truly a gift from God (Psa. 127:3).

To the elders at Oldham Lane.
Thank you for your leadership and friendship.

To all the writers of this book.
Thank you for your contribution,
not just to this project, but to the Kingdom.
I am blessed to know you and to work with you.

www.ingramcontent.com/pod-product-compliance
Lightning Source LLC
LaVergne TN
LVHW021346080426
835508LV00020B/2133